10/29/96

Administrative Computing in Higher Education

Issues in Enterprise-Wide Networks and Systems

Administrative Computing in Higher Education

Issues in Enterprise-Wide Networks and Systems

Les Lloyd, Editor

Information Today, Inc.
Medford, NJ
1996

Copyright© 1996 by: Information Today, Inc.
                                       143 Old Marlton Pike
                                       Medford, NJ 08055

Printed in the United States of America.

Administrative computing in higher education : issues in enterprise
   -wide networks and systems / edited by Les Lloyd.
        p.   cm.
     Includes bibliographical references and index.
     ISBN 1-57387-007-2 (hard cover)
     1. Universities and colleges—United States—Administration—Data
processing—Case studies.   I. Lloyd, Les.
LB2341.A329   1996
378.1'00285—dc20   95-51691
                                                                        CIP

Price: $39.50
Book Editor: James H. Shelton
Cover Design: Jeanne Wachter

DEDICATION

This book is dedicated to my niece Alexandra, and nephews Evan and Ryan, in the hope that by the time they are old enough to read such stuff, we'll have it all figured out!

Contents

PART ONE:

MOVING TO A NEW SYSTEM

PART TWO:

CLIENT/SERVER MODELS: DISTRIBUTING THE POWER

PART THREE:
USING OLDER SYSTEMS

PART FOUR:
LONG-RANGE PLANS

PREFACE

This project began in 1992 as a letter to colleagues interested in documenting their experiences in administrative computing. Two years and a new publisher later, we asked authors to revise their work based on what had happened in the intervening period. Today, their efforts show the experiences of computing departments in transition, whether updating legacy systems or converting to new hardware and software, offered in the hope that their accounts may serve as lessons (positive or negative) for those beginning or with projects in progress.

P<small>ART</small> O<small>NE</small>

Moving to a New System

Chapter One

IN CONTEMPLATION OF ADOPTING
A RELATIONAL DATABASE

Glenn A. Bieber
Assistant Director, Computer Services
Bloomsburg University

Robert J. Parrish
Vice President for Administration and University Treasurer
Bloomsburg University

Robert W. Abbott
Director of Academic Computing
Bloomsburg University

INTRODUCTION

Bloomsburg University is a public four-year institution of 8,000 students located in mideastern Pennsylvania. The student body is balanced evenly among majors in liberal arts, business, and teacher preparation/nursing. One of the strategic direction statements of the planning mission calls for integration of technology into the instructional programs.

The University now owns approximately 1,500 personal computers and several host systems, with the UNISYS 2200 serving as the administrative mainframe. About half of the personal computers are available to students, with two-thirds being IBM-compatible and the remainder Apple Macintosh. Each faculty member who desires a personal computer is provided a choice of an Apple product or IBM PC (or compatible) machine, along with access to the campus-wide, system-wide (State System of Higher Education net-work—SSHEnet), and worldwide (BITNET, PREPnet, Internet) networks. By the end of the 1992-93 academic year, Bloomsburg University would have 500 faculty and staff users hardwired to the network, not including networked classrooms, general purpose computer laboratories, and off-campus modem interfaces.

This case study outlines those issues under consideration as Bloomsburg University of Pennsylvania examines the prospect of moving from a hierarchical database on its UNISYS 2200/402 mainframe to a relational database.

THE COMPUTING ENVIRONMENT

Computer Services are split into two discrete functions at Bloomsburg, with both reporting to the vice president for administration. Academic Computing takes primary responsibility for local area networking, general instructional laboratories, networked classrooms, faculty computer applications and client/server relationships. Administrative Computing has primary responsibility for host computing, administrative databases, ethernet networks and network communications, administrative programming, library systems support, and administrative PC applications and service. This chapter deals primarily with administrative systems support databases, and the desire for change from the hierarchical database.

All major administrative systems run on the UNISYS, with 32 megabytes of main memory and 30 gigabytes of disk storage. Most of the administrative systems are written in Cobol, with database calls directed toward UNISYS' DMS 1100 hierarchical database. There are 1,600 active Cobol programs, comprised of 1.2 million lines of code, with an additional 700 programs written in QLP 1100, a query language. Administrative systems development began in the 1970s, and has evolved to the point where highly customized and integrated programs provide online data to all administrative and academic departments. Purchase requests and maintenance work orders are initiated by online screen transactions, and students schedule their own classes through networked PC laboratories. Faculty advisors may override class limits or prerequisites from their office PCs. During online scheduling, the center experiences 100,000 online transactions each day. The library uses a UNISYS PALS package that provides online catalog, acquisitions, and circulation data to networked personal computers, and the information is also available to off-campus students and the general public through modem interface.

In order to reduce the backlog of user-requested services, Computer Services implemented a UNISYS product called MAPPER in 1987. MAPPER is a fourth generation language that incorporates a database using tabled files. The goal at that time was to improve the productivity of the computer center staff. By providing a fourth generation language, end-user requests could be implemented in a more timely fashion. MAPPER also supports a set of commands that enables end-users to define and access data directly. Thus, users could produce their own simple reports and inquiry screens rather than depend on the computer center staff to create custom programs.

Several successful systems have been developed using the MAPPER database. However, only those requests that involved freestanding systems could be accomplished using MAPPER, because the majority of requests deal with enhancements to existing Cobol systems. Another approach MAPPER offers is the downloading of hierarchical databases to MAPPER files; by thus providing access to their data, users are able to query information directly. A good example of this technique is used by the Admissions Office. Information on applicants is loaded daily to a MAPPER version of items captured from the hierarchical database. The Admissions Office is then able to ask "What If" questions to determine which applicants should be accepted, based upon their criteria models.

On the whole, MAPPER has been a successful venture for Bloomsburg University; however, this programming language is not without limitations. MAPPER is a proprietary product and does not lend itself to the "Open Systems" concept. Another shortcoming is the extensive amount of computer resources required. To convert the current hierarchical databases to MAPPER would require a considerable increase of computer power and would further tie the University to a proprietary language and file structure. MAPPER also does not provide full life cycle CASE (Computer-Aided Software Engineering) or an integrated data dictionary.

Computer Services also had hoped that MAPPER's user-oriented command set would promote end-user computing. Although campus-wide and individual department training was provided by Computer Services, the use of the end-user commands has only been successful in a limited number of departments. The general feeling of Computer Services is that a more user-friendly interface will be required before University users will apply tools to directly access data.

In the summer of 1990, an independent evaluation of Computer Services was conducted. As a member of the Pennsylvania State System of Higher Education, each department at Bloomsburg University is required to participate every five years in an independent evaluation of facilities, services, and long-range planning. The University contracted the services of Douglas Bigelow of Wesleyan University and Philip Long of Yale University to perform the evaluation. Both evaluators hold director positions in computing at their respective universities and had performed computer and networking consultations for several universities in the past.

The final report of the evaluation presented recommendations for future direction of Computer Services and the University. Although not all the recommendations are pertinent to this case study, three of them directly apply. Computer Services must (1) migrate to more productive tools to support end-users more efficiently; (2) embrace and support distributed computing to empower end-users to address their less sophisticated needs directly; (3) adopt an applications life cycle to redesign and reimplement applications that have exceeded their "useful life."

Although the evaluation formally defined future direction for Computer Services, many of the recommendations coincided with the goals the department had been developing before the evaluation took place. Computer Services recognized the need to shift resources from a predominately mainframe environment to a distributed one. As a result of a University directive to develop a five-year plan within all departments, Computer Services formalized the long-term direction for the center. The plan incorporated both the recommendations of the independent evaluation and Computer Services' own goals.

Another factor that influenced the planning process was Computer Services' reliance upon proprietary hardware and software. Since all major applications are designed and implemented on the UNISYS mainframe, Computer Services believed the University to be in a vulnerable position, having no flexibility in pursuing outside software or hardware due to the high dependence upon UNISYS products. At the same time the plan was being developed, the UNISYS Corporation itself was struggling to become profitable while burdened with high debt. The risks of remaining with proprietary systems became even more obvious as the future of the UNISYS Corporation itself became an issue.

The following long-term goals pertinent to this case study were established:

1. Increase support of end-user computing by
   a. Implementing a university-wide database management system that will support multiple platforms and multiple levels of computers. This database management system would be used to design centralized systems as well as local office systems.
   b. Implementing an end-user, fourth generation language that would be used directly by campus users to develop their own ad hoc query language programs to view and print data.
2. Increase support of distributed computing by
   a. Implementing a database management system that provides distributed processing of data across platforms, operates in a networked environment, and supports the client/server methodology.
   b. Networking all campus offices with the capability to access centralized data or local data when appropriate.
   c. Establishing mid-size computers in large offices and high activity areas to process unique applications locally.
   d. Establishing a test environment separate from the production environment to minimize the impact of new development, enhancements, or maintenance activities on mission critical applications.
3. Increase current staff productivity by
   a. Implementing CASE tools to reduce the time required to design, program, and maintain applications software.

b. Implementing a database management system that provides an integrated data dictionary, rule-based field definition, and a fourth generation programming language to reduce the time required to program and maintain applications software.

c. Rewriting current applications or, by purchasing packaged software to replace current in-house developed software, to reduce the time required to enhance or maintain existing applications.

4. Reduce dependence on vendor hardware by

a. Implementing a database management system that supports the "Open Systems" concept. Particularly the premise that software written on one vendor's computer can be ported to another vendor's computer without totally rewriting the application.

b. Rewriting current programs or purchasing packaged application software to migrate applications from the current database.

c. Purchasing UNIX-based hardware as the preferred future computer for applications development and implementation.

In addition to the obvious benefits that the goals directly address, several additional gains are anticipated. By migrating from the mainframe to a UNIX environment, the University would have the option to "right size" computer applications. Although this advantage is definitely seen as long-term and would not be realized until all applications were rewritten, UNIX-based hardware gives the University a more desirable position for negotiating future purchases. Package solutions would become a more feasible choice. Rather than expending internal resources to develop new applications software, a package solution could be considered.

Currently, the pool of available software is limited to packages written for the UNISYS 2200. On the other hand, running UNIX based hardware opens the door to a larger number of alternative packages. The UNIX world is also experiencing growth in new offerings, while the UNISYS selection is static. A benefit that is hard to measure is the window that the plan will open to future technology. Although the UNISYS mainframe has been an excellent vehicle for developing online transaction processing systems, it is questionable whether many of the new technologies will interface with the current environment. PC-based front-ends, such as ToolBook or OracleCard, are not as compatible with mainframe processing as the client/server environment under a UNIX system. New technologies in the imaging and voice arenas are being developed outside the hierarchical database structure. Unless the University moves to alternative hardware, many of these technologies will be unavailable for future applications development.

OBSTACLES TO REACHING THE GOALS

Although Computer Services' managers agree that the plan to move to a relational database is sound and necessary for future growth of administrative systems, the road to accomplishing the goal has many obstacles. Each of these issues must be addressed and the appropriate strategy developed if the plan is to be successful. Some factors are briefly discussed here.

Contented End-users

Generally, campus end-users are quite satisfied with the administrative systems supported by Computer Services. The customized systems developed by the center have automated all the major functions performed by various offices across campus. Online response time is excellent, with minor increases experienced during student scheduling periods. The average campus end-user sees little need to change systems that work.

It is important to recognize that the root cause of this prospective change is significantly different from what have been the normal reasons one upgrades a computer or changes mainframe vendors. Usually, accumulated user need outstrips machine capability, making client demand the driving force in the decision to bring about change. In this instance, however, the users are basically satisfied, programs are quite good, and mainframe performance and reliability must be rated highly. At this point the end-users are not involved in the discussion and are probably not aware that a plan for a major conversion is being considered. As they are unaware and uninvolved in the discussion, they cannot be considered allies at this time. Bringing the end-users into the planning process should have at least two purposes: to get their input as to needs, and to educate them as to the prospective benefits. By holding seminars and having vendors give presentations, the end-user becomes aware of how some unarticulated problems could be solved or how some present office processes might be enhanced by the new technology.

The Rewrite of Existing Applications

A massive effort will be required to convert the current applications to a new database structure. With 1,600 Cobol programs and 700 query language programs in existence, the job seems staggering. Initial estimates range from three to five years of effort. Even considering a ten-fold increase in productivity predicted by some database management systems, Computer Services anticipates a major challenge.

To date no software has been found to perform conversion of Cobol programs from a hierarchical database to a relational structure. Even if conversion software is made available, some of the major benefits of moving toward a relational database would be lost. Conversion software is not likely to have the capability to convert code while creating an integrated dictionary or establishing CASE files.

Productivity gains, anticipated by implementing an integrated dictionary and CASE, would not be achieved.

An applications package solution also is not a promising alternative. Packages that have been investigated do not support all the functionality and custom design of the current systems. Users would not accept anything less. Especially critical is the online student scheduling module. Package solutions would not support this application without major modifications. Although some areas such as Human Resources or Financial applications may be candidates for package solutions, further investigation is required.

Existing System Status Quo Period

During a rewrite, users would be forced to accept a status quo period for requesting enhancements to existing applications. Any directives made upon the University which require immediate computer support would divert conversion resources and adversely affect the rewrite schedule.

Dual Systems

For the period of the rewrite both the hierarchical and relational database systems would co-exist. Expertise and maintenance to both systems would definitely stretch the current personnel resources of Computer Services. Licensing and maintenance fees would be duplicative during this period.

Re-education of Personnel

In order to develop applications under a relational database structure, the entire systems and programming staff would need to be retrained. Development using an SQL language, CASE tools, and a client/server structure are all foreign to most of the current staff. Realignment and reclassification of the staff may also be required.

The Library System

The library package runs on the UNISYS 2200 hardware using UNISYS' proprietary hierarchical database. A rewrite of the library system is not a feasible solution. Computer Services' lack of time and expertise to develop a library system in-house was a contributing factor in purchasing the current library package.

A possible alternative may be to remain with the library package but downsize it to a midsize UNISYS computer. Other institutions have taken this approach. In fact, two sister universities in the Pennsylvania State System of Higher Education have purchased midsize UNISYS computers used solely to run the UNISYS library system. A library computer and attendant maintenance and operational costs would also be a consideration.

Being on the Front Line

Although information management trade magazines seem to cite numerous examples of corporate organizations downsizing from mainframes to UNIX, instances of universities rewriting existing satisfactory applications have not been found. Several universities are downsizing their administrative systems by taking the purchased package solution, but their hierarchical database systems were weak or limited, which provided the impetus for change. To date, not one University that has rewritten its applications from a hierarchical to a relational database has been established.

In the past, Bloomsburg University has been a leader in the Pennsylvania State System of Higher Education in installing new technology, developing administrative systems, and implementing campus networks. However, the move to an entirely new application development technology will be a challenge to sell on campus. The fact that other universities are not making a similar transition compounds the task.

Cost

The Administrative Computer Services Director estimates transitional costs to amount to $900,000 over a four-year period. The amount covers the acquisition of database management software, some hardware, and training, but does not address conversion of the 2,300 current programs or the library system. If purchased packages are the solution, costs could amount to $2 million, plus continuing maintenance and licensing fees on the purchased systems.

PREPARATION FOR OPEN SYSTEMS

Since staff expertise has been focused historically on supporting a mainframe environment, Computer Services felt that key personnel should be educated toward the direction of the long-term plan. The broad goals required detailed refinement. In order to accomplish this task, the staff needed to become technically competent in UNIX administration and relational database technology.

UNIX has been a presence in academic computing since the mid-eighties. At that time, the Business Computer & Information Systems Department shifted academic instruction from the mainframe environment to an AT&T based UNIX machine. Computer Services' first production experience with UNIX was with a UNISYS 6000/50 purchased to serve as a networking device for the library PALS system. In order to prepare for the installation, a member of the staff was given the additional responsibility of UNIX administrator; the UNIX administrator attended several extensive UNIX classes offered by UNISYS to prepare for the assignments.

Computer Services management also felt that if UNIX was to be a possible alternative to the mainframe, additional staff would require training. A group of nine staff members were chosen for the training; this same group was involved with the installation of a new campus-wide ethernet network for the University, where UNIX experience would also be desirable. The chairperson of the Business Computer & Information Systems Department consented to provide a condensed version of a UNIX class which is given to majors in the Computer Science curriculum. From this initial class, and through on-the-job learning, Computer Services now supports a UNISYS 6000/65, a UNISYS 6000/60, a SUN workstation, and an experimental UNIX-based workstation. Processing on the more powerful UNISYS UNIX machines primarily provides mainframe emulation capabilities. MS-DOS and Macintosh personal computers connected to the University network are able to access the UNISYS mainframe by connecting to the UNIX computers. Emulation software residing on the UNIX machines translates to the proper protocol to enable the PCs to emulate a UNISYS terminal. This provides a cheaper alternative to PC resident software. Computer Services' expertise in the field of UNIX has increased dramatically in the last one to two years. The center is currently in a positive posture for moving ahead toward "Open Systems" solutions based on UNIX technology.

In order to better understand and to place Computer Services in a position where the Center could intelligently recommend a future relational database for the University, Computer Services began an evaluation of available Relational Database Management Systems (RDMS). The Database Administrator was given the task of becoming knowledgeable in relational database technology, developing criteria to select an RDMS, and narrowing available RDMS packages to the best choice for the requirements at Bloomsburg. The approach that was developed included: 1) training in relational database for the database administrator, 2) developing criteria for selection, 3) contacting RDMS vendors for information on their package, 4) narrowing the field to three or four packages, and 5) evaluating the final candidates to select the best RDMS for the University. Both the database administrator and several management staff attended seminars offered by various RDMS vendors to become more familiar with relational databases. The database administrator also attended independent classes on relational databases that were not vendor sponsored. The strategy here was that unbiased courses on relational databases would allow the evaluation to proceed without prejudice.

The criteria for evaluating RDMS packages was divided into two categories, the first being requirements that were deemed mandatory. Failure to meet any of the mandatory requirements would constitute an unacceptable RDMS for Bloomsburg University's needs. The second category consisted of criteria that were considered to be desirable but their absence would not eliminate an RDMS candidate. The criteria developed is presented as follows.

Mandatory Criteria

The RDMS must:

1. Run under the UNIX operating system to support Computer Services' goal of becoming vendor independent.

2. Incorporate ANSI Structured Query Language (SQL) to promote end-user computing for campus offices, and to reduce application development time and resources required for development of future systems.
3. Support the access to and integrity of distributed databases through local area networks.
4. Provide Online Transaction Processing (OLTP) serving multiple users with full online backup and recovery capabilities.
5. Interface with CASE tools or provide CASE tools as a product with the RDMS package to reduce applications development and maintenance time and resources.
6. Provide an integrated data dictionary to reduce applications development and maintenance time and resources.

Desirable Criteria

The RDMS should:

1. Run under additional operating systems such as UNISYS' OS 1100 or MS-DOS.
2. Have available applications software packages that will encompass some or all of the University's current custom applications.
3. Interface with other software packages in order to share data. These include spreadsheet generators, work processors, graphic generators, desktop publishers, and other databases.
4. Be supported by a reliable vendor who provides product support, training support, and stability in the marketplace.
5. Provide ease of use to both campus end-users and the staff of Computer Services.
6. Be easy to learn and to adapt to the University's requirements.
7. Provide tools to convert the University's existing applications to the relational database environment.

After the criteria were established and approved within Computer Services, contacts were made with six RDMS vendors. Responses from the vendors varied in the amount of information received and support they were willing to supply toward the evaluation. From the information gathered, the field of candidates was narrowed to three.

The major segment of the evaluation consisted of developing the same system under a version of each vendor's RDMS. An actual end-user requested project was used. All requirements for the project were previously developed. The project itself had also been implemented under the MAPPER system. The testing of each RDMS involved establishing the database, creating input and output screens, and building the programs to load the initial database. Execution of menu and report generators, as well as the various methods available for executing queries were performed. After completion of the testing phase, the RDMS was evaluated against established criteria.

As a result of the evaluation, the Oracle RDMS became the highest ranking package of the three evaluated. It was the only product that satisfied all the mandatory criteria, and also appeared to be superior in areas of CASE tools and integrated data dictionary. The applications development tools that Oracle's suite of products offers was found to be more comprehensive than the other vendors. The integrated data dictionary feature allows menus, forms, reports and queries to be built via full screen menus with point and click technology. This feature greatly increases the productivity of any staff member producing menus or forms. The integrated CASE technology of Oracle would also be a major benefit in developing and maintaining applications.

Within the desirable criteria, Oracle also outperformed the other two RDMS packages. Oracle is also clearly the leader in the number of applications packages available. In addition, a version of Oracle was recently developed to run under the OS 1100 UNISYS operating system; although this version is currently in the testing mode, it does offer options for future consideration.

Another factor purposely not considered in either the mandatory or desirable criteria also reinforces the preference of Oracle: the Business Computer & Information Systems under the College of Business teaches Oracle database development as a major part of its curriculum. Future liaisons between the Business Computer & Information Systems Department and Computer Services could have mutual benefits for both areas. Oracle would be a common component between the two areas for sharing technology and learning experiences. Computer Services could also serve as a source of internships and class projects in the Oracle field.

FUTURE STRATEGIES

Weighing all the benefits, obstacles, and planning involved with a major transition from hierarchical database to relational database technology, the likelihood of implementing a relational database in the immediate future is doubtful. Preliminary estimates over a four-year period show a cost of nearly one million dollars at the least. The cost includes purchasing the RDMS, a UNIX computer capable of processing the University's transaction throughput, development workstations and formal classes for Computer Services staff.

A special opportunity exists. We have no compelling reasons to change our administrative computing hardware and software, as both are reliable. The hardware can be expanded to meet all needs for the foreseeable future. The UNISYS hardware will be owned by the University in two years, after which a considerable yearly savings will result that can be redirected toward future systems/hardware acquisitions. We have time to engage in extensive reviews of hardware, operating systems, databases, networking and decentralized computing schemes. We may eventually change not only a database and hardware, but our whole concept of administrative computing. The posture is rather one of positioning the University for the future. In that light, the best alternative at this time may be to continue to move in the relational database direction in a conservative manner. A more conservative transition plan would expand the implementation timeframe, thereby reducing the risk factor as well as the impact on the end-users.

Before committing the University to a long-term relational database solution, a phased transition plan such as the one suggested below should be adopted. Each phase provides checkpoint reviews that require approvals before the next phase is undertaken. The initial commitment of the phased approach is minimal but increases progressively though each phase as the University becomes more committed to the transition. Major budget and resources commitments are deferred until after the last phase is approved.

Although Computer Services is responsible for the major effort, a task force functions as the reviewing body to determine the success or failure of each phase. The task force comprises a cross-section of the University population, including student representation. The task force presents the findings of each phase and recommends continuing or dissolving the transition plan. Actual approval of a relational database solution ultimately rests with the President's Cabinet. As each phase of the transition plan is completed, however, several campus committees—the Administrative Computer Advisory, Academic Computer Advisory and Campus-wide Technology Committees— will approve continuation or dissolution.

THE PHASED TRANSITION PLAN

Phase I—Develop a Functional Model

Process: A functional model is developed to demonstrate the capabilities of a relational database. The model consists of a small portion of the existing student system with comparable online displays and update transactions as exist under the current system.

Total Development Time: 3 to 6 months

Required Resources:	Database Administrator	40 work days
	Training	15 work days
	MS-DOS 486 PC	
	RDMS and related software	
Hardware, Software, and Training Costs:	Training	$3,000
	MS-DOS 486 PC	$3,000
	RDMS and related software	$2,000
	TOTAL	$8,000

Deliverables: A presentation of the online displays and updates using the functional model is presented to the task force. Interested campus users are invited as well. Demonstrations of available development tools are also shown.

Approval/Rejection: The task force evaluates the differences between the functional model and the comparable existing functions under the current environment. Development tools are also compared to the existing development methods. The task force recommends whether (1) relational technology meets the University's long-term goals, and (2) the relational transition is one the University should further pursue.

Phase II—Develop a Pilot Project

Process: An end-user submitted request is selected, with the approval of the requesting department, as a pilot project to be developed using relational database technology. The project is restricted to a limited user base. The purchase of a UNIX server will be diverted to other uses if the plan does not extend beyond Phase II. Additional resources will be necessary to rewrite the application using the existing development environment if, at the conclusion of this phase, the plan is discontinued.

Total Development Time: 6 months to 1 year

Required Resources:	Programmer/Analyst	135 work days
	Database Administrator	80 work days
	UNIX Administrator	10 work days
	Training	15 work days
	MS-DOS 486 PC	
	UNIX server	
	RDMS software (16 total users)	

(Assumes a network connection exists for involved users.)

Hardware, Software, and Training Costs:	Training	$2,000
	MS-DOS 486 PC	$2,500
	UNIX server	$40,000
	RDMS software	$35,000
	TOTAL	$79,500

Potential Pilot System: The Transfer Evaluation System automates the validation and acceptance of transfer credits for students transferring courses from an outside university. Campus users of the system include the offices of Admissions, Registrar, and selected academic departments.

Deliverables: A production version of the system is implemented and used by the participating offices for at least three months.

Approval/Rejection: The task force evaluates the success or failure of the project through input obtained from both the end-users and Computer Services. Major consideration is given to end-user satisfaction and ease of development. The task force recommends to the committees whether to continue or end the transition plan.

Phase III—Develop a Campus-wide Project

Process: An existing application, that effects numerous departments across the University, is rewritten using the relational database. The project selected must expose campus users to features of relational database technology that are to be evaluated. The upgrade of the UNIX server will be diverted to other uses if the plan does not extend beyond Phase III.

Total Development Time: 6 months to 1 year

Required Resources:	Programmer/Analyst	180 work days
	Database Administrator	80 work days
	UNIX Administrator	15 work days
	Advanced training	200 work days
	UNIX server upgrade	
	RDMS software upgrade (16 concurrent users)	

(Assumes a network connection exists for involved users.)

Hardware, Software, and Training Costs:	Advanced training	$3,000
	UNIX server upgrade	$15,000
	RDMS software upgrade	$35,000
	TOTAL	$53,000

Potential Campus-wide System: A subset of the Student System is rewritten to encompass Residence Life update transactions and campus-wide student information queries. The system requires a two-way feed to maintain the existing Student System with Residence Life data and to update the relational system with pertinent data from Student System. Campus users of the system include all offices that query the system for student information and particularly the Residence Life Office, which will be performing update functions.

Deliverables: A production version of the existing system is implemented and used by campus departments for at least 3 months.

Approval/Rejection: The task force performs an intensive evaluation of the system. User interviews and questionnaires are developed and conducted. The task force makes their recommendations to the committees.

Phase IV—Develop a Conversion Schedule and Associated Cost

Process: Computer Services, in conjunction with the task force, develops a schedule to rewrite existing hierarchical systems to the relational database environment. Rewriting of existing systems is anticipated to cover a time frame of 3 to 5 years. Associated costs of software and hardware may be prorated across this time frame or incurred on the outset. This decision will reflect the best cost alternative at the time. Additional personnel to accomplish the task will also be considered. Options may include temporary employees during the rewrite time frame with the possibility of full-time employment through attrition.

Total Development Time: 3 months

Deliverables: A comprehensive plan to rewrite all existing hierarchical systems is developed. The plan documents schedules, associated costs, and personnel requirements.

Approval/Rejection: The task force presents the schedule and associated costs to the committees and President's Cabinet for approval to begin the conversion process.

SUMMARY

As information technology evolves, it is imperative that organizations upgrade to hardware, operating systems, and database management systems that support future technological advancements. Bloomsburg University has made substantial investments for the future in areas such as networking and desktop computing. In the area of administrative computing, however, the University must begin a transition from an environment based in proprietary hardware and a hierarchical database to a relational database supportive of "Open Systems" concepts. This direction will eventually be necessitated by end-user requirements that will result in the need to incorporate e-mail, imaging, voice, and video into more traditional administrative transactions. A prudent transition plan will provide the time necessary to train staff, gain experience, reduce the risk factor, and attain campus acceptance of the transition. Reengineering mature administrative applications is a formative task requiring years to accomplish. Given the magnitude of the undertaking, implementation of the transition plan should begin directly.

CHAPTER TWO

DISTRIBUTING THE DATA

Dorothy H. Hess
President
POISE Users Group

INTRODUCTION

New and developing Networking Technology has created unlimited opportunities on university campuses for sharing administrative data. The key to this sharing is cooperation—between and among staff members who have access to the technology and the data it supports.

At Scripps, since we're such a small institution, we could provide many of these opportunities before networking technology was prominent. In 1985, at Scripps, application packages were purchased for the traditional administrative offices—Admissions and Recruiting, Registration and Student Records, Billing and Receivables, (with Housing and Meal Plan information), Financial Aid, and Alumni and gift tracking in the Development office. These packages were all based on flat-file systems using a centralized DMS (data management system). Data could easily be transferred between office databases and each database could be referenced by any of the others. They were all centralized on a VAX and to this date there is no downloading into PCs. Each database has been as current as the office is able or willing to provide.

DATA FLOW

The purchased package for the Admission Office provides for entering data on perspective students who have made any kind of inquiry about attending the college. The recruiting process is tracked and all information is entered that provides the information the staff needs to make a decision regarding the student's admission.

When a new applicant registers for the first time, the system pulls appropriate data into the registration system so that she can be enrolled in classes.

Simultaneously, financial aid is being awarded. Upon completion of the registration process, the student can either take a bill generated by the registrar's office to the cashier, or the cashier can generate the bill.

The generated bill includes all charges and aid credits, including housing and mealcharges plus any miscellaneous charges or credits necessary. If a student has arranged for paying on an installment plan, appropriate calculations are made. All charges for off-campus study and housing programs have already been submitted to the bursar to be included on the bill. Receivables can be posted on a regular basis into the General Ledger.

At Scripps, the initial bill is generated in July before the student enrolls. This disallows the above initiation of the process in the registrar's office. Since a new student has not enrolled in particular classes, she is charged the anticipated full-time tuition. In order to provide appropriate information for billing, the computing center disperses necessary information electronically to the following offices: Billing, Registrar, Housing, Financial Aid, Development, Alumnae. This is done biweekly throughout the summer as new applicants state their intentions to attend Scripps.

The Development Office is provided with parent information for all the new students, allowing it to involve the parents in on-campus activities. The office can also begin to cultivate prospects whose children hava not requested financial aid—a healthy sign for fund raisers. The newly enrolled student becomes part of the Alumna database in order to track pertinent on-campus information.

THE ENTERPRISE PLAN

Having the departmental database available on every desktop has created havoc among office staff members. When everyone in the office has access to the same information, roles become muddled. Previously it was the responsibility of a clerk to enter data; now anyone in the office can update address or phone information.

It has become evident that many offices have been obtaining information from or about students. Who should now have the role of updating the database and what really is the latest information?

The Housing office may think it has the latest telephone number, but in a conversation the student just informed the billing office she has a new number, so the clerk immediately updated the database. The assistant in the Housing office did not hear the conversation so she changed it back thinking the database was outdated. It certainly wasn't the number she had on file. She had no way of knowing that the billing office had just entered it at the student's request.

Such processes have to be organized, not only within offices, but within the institution. Many people within many offices used to be responsible for updating their own databases, now one can handle it more efficiently.

No one now has to request information of one individual and wait for the results. The information is available on every desktop, not only within the office but in other offices where the information is needed.

The president can view a screen, listing the new applicants, or gifts to the college. SAT scores from the admissions office are available when she requests them in order to make top-level management decisions. Any particular office or staff member has lost "ownership" of the data. It has now become available where it is most needed on a timely basis.

Change has become the issue. It alters the power bases and comfort zones of people. We in the computing center continue to look at becoming developers of a campus-wide information system. Instead of overseeing the process of computerizing office tasks, we study the functions and processes of the institution and support them with appropriate technology.

A list of such functions may be as follows:

- marketing the institution for recruits and their parents
- enrolling students and maintaining transcripts
- providing an environment for growth and development
- generating necessary funds
- educating students.

IS leaders need to gain a thorough understanding of each of these functions in order to guide technical decisions that drive the processes while computing center staff look at the tasks required to meet the above objectives. The tasks are not being completed by any given office staff but among a team of interoffice personnel.

The function of generating funds, for example, entails many different tasks within avariety of departments. The major purpose of a development office is to generate large funding sources along with ongoing annual gifts. Student receivables and the financial aid office serve these ends within the student sector.

The student bill is generated according to information gathered from a variety of sources—admission fees, enrolled courses, housing and meal costs, medical services, parking and vehicle registration fees, and the library. The financial aid officer determines which students are to receive scholarship funds generated through gifts to the college.

The gift accounting system feeds directly into the General Ledger, with scholarship gifts also feeding into the financial aid funds. A record of who receives how much scholarship money from The Sir Donald Duck Foundation is made available to the appropriate development officer so that an event can be planned, perhaps, where the recipients can meet with Sir Donald.

All of these offices need to have parts of a student database resident, which then feed into the receivables system and from there into the General Ledger.

The business office performs the traditional tasks of investing and/or assisting in the budgetary disbursement of gifts to the college and the tuition payments from students. Personnel/human resources assumes the responsibility of assuring a viable income to employees of the college.

Another source of funds, not considered traditional, is the Admissions Office which often prefers to enroll students who request no financial aid. These efforts don't feed into any accounting system, but the data is highly regarded within the development office.

The office of Public Relations and Communications performs the major duties of marketing the institution, another major function of the college. How does a person whose responsibility it is to direct Public Relations provide leadership and control over all the material that is sent off-campus when word processors and laser printers populate the desktops of every office.

The director of computing, the IS leader, needs to work closely with the Director of Public Relations. The computing department is aware of who uses, or is capable of creating certain types of documents because its staff knows who has what technology and training. If there is to be any quality control, the two directors need to work closely together and with everyone who is involved.

Sometimes the first to recognize these information matrices or needs arethe Information Systems people. Requests for data or information come through our office. And it is our responsibility to help the users determine their precise information needs to be able to perform within the Institution Plan.

In a small institution, the director or CIO assumes this role. This person needs to be in close contact with persons from the administrative offices. She needs to find out the activities of the offices; then use her knowledge of current trends in technology to become the thought leader in providing resources that respond to these needs.

RESPONSIBILITIES OF THE COMPUTING CENTER

We are increasingly more aligned with being an information utility and less of a source for developing new programs. Our role is becoming one of training users, analyzing data flow patterns, and generally improving service functions. As we do, we become an effective tool for strategic management and decision making.

Planning within centralized computing operations now provides for offices or departments to support some of their own information needs. We spend less time programming and more time supporting users. More importantly, we provide the technology needed to share important data on a timely basis between offices.

For example if a registrar chooses to purchase the capability to track retention statistics, she should be allowed that capability. The staff in the computing center has no responsibility in this process except to provide for these statistics to be networked to other offices needing the data.

In order to support these needs more effectively, the IS director needs to find out *who* needs the information, in *what* form, *how often*, and *when*. She guides thepurchasing so that any new resources meet whatever connectivity is required. Most users are unaware of the technological requirements needed to allow this sharing to happen.

If the data needs to interface with other software, the IS director asks *why?*. That question may be asked to find out what format the data must take. The IS staff's responsibility, then, is to network data. If we don't have the knowledge of how to do that, we know where to go to find out.

More important, and even more difficult, are the processes of networking the people and managing the data on the system. How do we find out for whom to make the data available—and when and how they need it.

How do we get the answers to these questions? We need to learn the business of administering a college, how to plan a budget, develop strategies, and develop an overall comprehension of the functions of the institution. Technical expertise is no longer sufficient.

Continuing conversations or meetings may determine that minor concessions are necessary on the part of either the user or the computing director in order to sufficiently meet the need, yet save some investment dollars in the purchase of new programs. Such communications, the interactions between users and computing staff, not only create more efficient programs and overall technology resources deployment, but also force improved management of all processes. This eventually meets the needs of the basic institutional functions.

IS staff have not been trained in process management. We need to work closely with users, not against them. When nontraditional information is generated in traditional offices, or when information is needed in nontraditional forms or in some offices that "shouldn't need it," the problem becomes one of education.

The task becomes one of training users to think differently. The data in their office is not "theirs;" it is an asset of the institution. And only when it is allowed to become an asset will the investment in computing resources pay for itself and become a tool in strategic planning.

At Scripps, any PC or local package must be approved by the computing director before a department can purchase it. This process of managing resources serves to assure not only supportability, but also efficient portability and connectivity. The approval process provides an opportunity for both the requesting office or department and the computing director to learn to know the expectations and requirements of the functions of the college.

Networking the users is probably the greatest single challenge for IS people. Actually it's a whole new concept. We have been trained to insure the reliability of computing resources, not manage people. Most technology can not be purchased "off the shelf," so our role changes to one of supporting users. Then, to establish these resources as strategic planning devices, we become thought leaders as these changes occur.

> Within the next ten years, both the structure of organizations and the jobs of the senior people within organizations will be drastically changed primarily because of information . . . ."

—(Peter Drucker)

CHAPTER THREE

CABLING ON CAMPUS

Timothy Henry Tracy
Associate Director of Computing Services
Columbia College

One of the first considerations in a computer migration is the process by which access to the new system will be obtained. The most obvious solution is a local area network (LAN). A LAN network, by definition, limits communications to a relatively small geographical area. With the increase in technology and standardization, a LAN can be designed in an unlimited number of ways. A person needs no technical expertise when planning a LAN. This chapter addresses the use of fiber optic cabling and how it can be utilized in designing a local area network.

Today fiber optic cabling is common terminology. Businesses such as telephone and cable television companies have realized the potential of fiber optic cabling. One advantage is its resistance to lightning damage. Another advantage is that it allows the transmission of data signals from an entire building through one pair of fiber cable. College and University administrators should also use fiber optic cabling. The usual campus configuration of buildings widespread over a fairly large area offers a unique opportunity for fiber optic technology.

Every campus is unique as to what buildings should be connected and what persons should have access to the network. There are many considerations when planning a fiber network layout.

The network designer should be familiar with conduit runs on campus as well as any existing cabling configurations (existing cables might possibly be used in a fiber optic network). The locations around campus that need to be connected to the network and the number of users at each location should be established. The designer should be aware of the capabilities of the computer systems to which the fiber network will be connected as well as be acquainted with the physical layout of the campus, new additions and any necessary renovations to existing buildings. Future expansion is a primary consideration in a network due to the potential increase in the number of users and building sites requiring access to administrative computers and the need to integrate administrative systems with others computers campus-wide.

The network covered in this chapter is now being used on the campus at Columbia College of South Carolina. Columbia College is a four-year private college for women, with an enrollment of approximately 1200 students. The primary function of this network is to serve administrative users, yet it will serve as the basis for an integrated network. Academic concerns can be addressed piece by piece as necessary or when funding becomes available.

Faculty advisors will need access to the network during pre-registration. The network can be expanded to include dormitories through additional fiber cable runs. Other computer systems can also be added.

Administrative offices are located in several buildings on campus. The main Administrative building houses the President's Office, Financial Aid, Registrar, Business Office, and Computer Services. Student Services, Admissions, Alumnae/Development as well as Supply are all located in separate buildings (see Figure 3.1). The College took advantage of recent renovations to these buildings to wire them with unshielded twisted-pair cable for data communications. Each building wired has twisted-pair cable running from the user's work area to a central location in the building. Any new buildings would also have twisted-pair cable connected in this same manner. A central location in each building needs to be accessible for fiber optic cable. The fiber cable should be configured so as to connect back to the concentrator. It is preferred that the fiber cable run underground to the concentrator. There may be problems to overcome with obtaining this type of access to the concentrator, such as running additional conduit for the fiber. This method will reduce maintenance costs for the fiber cable.

Once the designer becomes familiar with the aforementioned issues, then consideration of the choice of a concentrator and its location must be made. The concentrator, or "star" as it is commonly known, will serve to link the main computer system through the cable runs. With a star configuration, all fiber runs on campus lead to a central point on campus. Although the computer center seems the logical location for the concentrator, a viable solution is a central location on campus. From this central location, it is only necessary to run one fiber pair to the computer. The main advantage of a star configuration is its capability to expand. With this type of configuration, any additional building can be connected to the network by running fiber from the building to an available port on the concentrator. A star configuration should reduce the distance of fiber cable runs on a campus. With the concentrator centrally located, it will never be necessary to run cable from one side of the campus to the other. This will also help in meeting the diameter requirements of the concentrator. Another advantage is that a fault in a cable run affects only that section of the network.

Choosing the right concentrator is an important decision. A primary concern is its expansion for future use. The concentrator should accommodate additional modules to connect more cables. We started with one four-port module, which allows the connection of three buildings. One port is necessary to connect a fiber pair to the server located in the computer center. We have the capability of installing fifteen more modules, which gives us the possibility of connecting over sixty pairs of fiber to the concentrator. With only one pair necessary per building, we have a wide margin of expansion.

The concentrator should also be able to accept modules that support twisted-pair and coaxial cable. This will allow different types of media to be connected to the concentrator. A twisted-pair module will take up one slot and support eight to twelve users. The concentrator should support Token Ring, Ethernet, and FDDI networks. It should also be able to transmit signals over the longest run of fiber cable on campus. There are many considerations when calculating the diameter requirements, such as the number of splices in a cable, whether the splices are fusion or mechanical, the number of light interface units to which the cable is to be connected, and the grade of the cable chosen. It is also important to note that a fusion splice will have lower power loss, but is more costly. The specifications for determining the maximum distances for a concentrator can be obtained from the manufacturer. The main computer connected to the network example used in this chapter is a DEC 5500 which runs a version of the UNIX operating system. The computer is located in an administrative building, but the users in that building do not have to go through the concentrator. Since the building is wired with twisted pair cable, the cable connects to a terminal server that connects to the same server as the concentrator.

To make future expansion of the fiber network as versatile and inexpensive as possible, the College installed light interface units in each building through which fiber cable passes. These units allow the flexibility of swapping fiber cables without splicing them. The fiber cable is terminated with standard ST connectors at both ends, allowing action similar to plugging and unplugging a telephone jack. This set-up will be very beneficial if there are any future additions or changes to the location of users requiring network access. It may be possible to use fiber cable already installed. Cable would have to be run only from the nearest light interface unit to the new location, which should also reduce the number of splices needed.

A communications center should be located in each building that is connected to the network. The center can be a closet or wall that is accessible for the cable. All work areas should have twisted-pair cable pulled to the communications center. The fiber optic cable from the concentrator should also lead to the communications center. The fiber cable will connect to a fiber optic transceiver at this location. The purpose of the transceiver is to convert the light signals to data signals. The fiber cable will have a transmit fiber and receive fiber. The transmit fiber at one end should connect to a receive port at the other end. The transceiver will then connect to a bridge that is attached to a terminal server. The bridge will allow the local area network to be portioned into a number of smaller LANs. The terminal server will allow users to access the computer to establish work sessions. The terminal servers that we use will allow eight ports per module with a capacity of seven modules, which allows a total of fifty-six users. Additional terminal servers can be added if necessary. The existing twisted-pair cable connects to the terminal server by a short jumper cable that is also made from twisted-pair cable. This allows the capability to adjust what module the user will be using. Another jumper cable plugs into a wall jack located at the user's work area, which connects to a serial interface that connects to a serial port at the user's terminal. This type of configuration is used with all buildings connected to the LAN (see Figure 3.2).

There are other issues to consider in planning a LAN. With the increased use of PC networks on campuses, it will be beneficial to connect any file servers to the concentrator. If the file server is using a concentrator, a fiber cable can link it with another concentrator. In the future we will connect the Leadership Center to the LAN (see Figure 3.1). The Leadership Center is a state-of-the-art teaching environment. This building has its own PC LAN to assist in classroom training. Its file server will be connected by fiber cable to the concentrator. Future expansion will include connecting student computer laboratories as well as the library system.

A reliable source should be located to pull the fiber cable and terminate it. The building services department of the College pulled the fiber cable. The terminations were contracted out. As the network grows in size and complexity, the chance of failure increases. To minimize the effect of a fault, backup procedures can be initiated. Because cable breaks are the most common problems in a network, it will be beneficial to run backup cables. The cost of running backup fiber cables is minimal compared to the amount spent on the LAN. Backup cables can be configured to switch over immediately in case of failure. A backup concentrator is also an option with a star configuration but carries a significant cost. A UPS (uninterruptible power supply) is also an option against power failures.

Once the network is online, there is minimal time spent maintaining the hardware. The LAN in this chapter illustrates the layout of cabling on campus and is not specific to the computer connected to it. The cost of the network covered in this case study is itemized in Table 3.1. Any education discounts the College received are reflected in these figures, which represent the cost of the hardware connected to the LAN. Other costs include hardware installation, fiber cable, and pulling and splicing of the fiber cable. Figure 3.1 represents a layout of the LAN used as an example in this chapter.

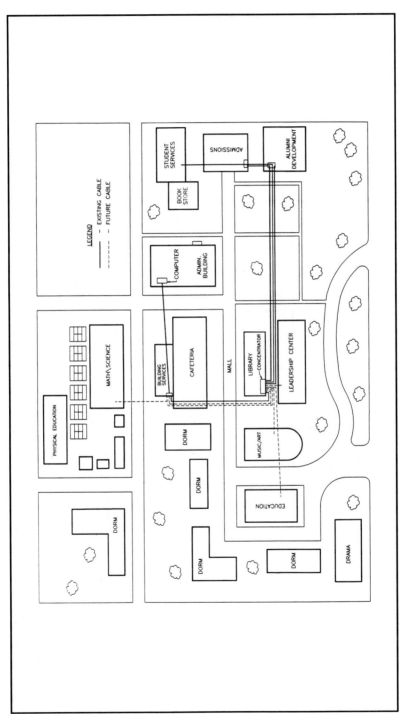

Figure 3.1 LAN Layout at Columbia College

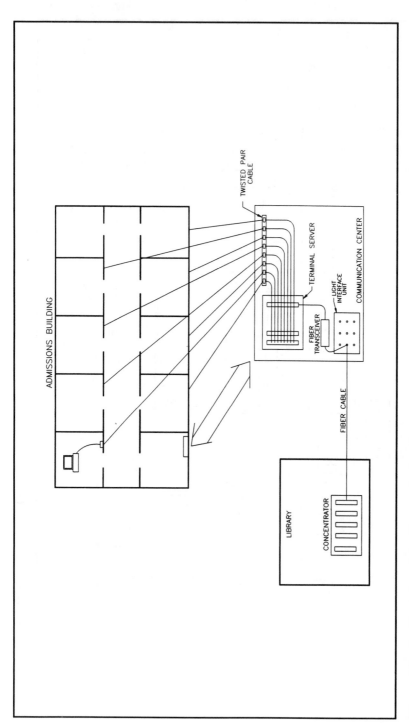

Figure 3.2 Configuration of the Communication Center

Table 3.1   Network Costs

LIBRARY: (LOCATION OF CONCENTRATOR)

concentrator	4,275.00	
fiber module	1,800.00	
		6,075.00

ALUMNAE/DEVELOPMENT:

fiber transceiver	535.50	
extension cable	45.50	
2 terminal servers	1,925.00	
hub	740.60	
bridge	2,290.40	
		5,537.00

ADMISSIONS:

fiber transceiver	535.50	
extension cable	45.50	
2 terminal servers	1,925.00	
hub	740.60	
bridge	2,290.40	
		5,537.00

STUDENT SERVICES:

fiber transceiver	535.50	
cable	56.00	
terminal server	1,071.00	
repeater	838.60	
		2,501.10

	============
TOTAL	$ 19,650.10

CHAPTER FOUR

MIGRATING FROM HOME-GROWN TO COMMERCIAL ADMINISTRATIVE COMPUTING SOFTWARE: DON'T FORGET THE PEOPLE!

John R. Luthy
Coordinator of Administrative Computing
Dickinson College

Hey, we did it, and we're still alive! We've left behind our familiar and comfortable world of home-grown Cobol systems for a commercial package and a new UNIX machine.

Through this chapter, I want to share not just the process but also the human side of our odyssey, because so far we've been successful. Research and discussion with experienced colleagues helped us develop plans and procedures focused on the mechanics of implementation. All too often the guidance stopped there. The human dynamics—unsettling effects of change, long hours, working under pressure alongside veteran and new staff—are just as important to anticipate for the successful implementation of a new system.

So let's review how Dickinson College:

- realized the need for change
- identified the campus-wide requirements
- developed a detailed Request for Proposal document
- identified budgetary requirements
- selected the software package
- selected the hardware platform
- established committees worth their weight in gold
- reorganized and expanded its staffing
- developed a data security plan
- communicates on- and off-campus like never before.

These accomplishments represent elements in a procedure. But people enact procedures! Woven throughout is a whole community of people both old and new to the college. As we look at each process, we'll also reflect on its human aspects.

BACKGROUND

Over 200 years old, Dickinson College is a four-year, private, liberal arts college with a student body of about 2000. In 1976, the first interactive, computer-based, administrative system went up. By 1981, most administrative functions involved some degree of computer-based data or programming. We were forced to replace the original minicomputer, which by that time ran the original student records system, a host of home-grown Cobol systems, a campus-wide word processor, and electronic mail.

GROWING PAINS

In 1982, Dickinson added a second minicomputer with a newer architecture, which in short order supported electronic mail and two major home-grown systems for alumni/development and the library's automated card catalog. Our financial aid and endowment management Cobol systems migrated from the old to the new machine. Although the first wave of microcomputer-based word processing took some of the pressure off the minicomputers, with each budget cycle additional terminals and microcomputers were meted out to increase desktop access to these administrative systems.

But intractable problems began to appear. The student records system was incapable of storing data for more than one academic year. The general purpose record maintenance program had reached the maximum program size supported by the computer's architecture. Response time was noticeably slow during peak periods of activity. All too often, we reached the maximum number of jobs, preventing someone from accessing a database, word processor, or electronic mail. Despite periodically transferring data from one system to another, most offices maintained independent files, at a cost of redundant human effort and computing resources, and inconsistent data. The campus computing community expected more.

TO BUY—BIG DECISION #1

The internal development of new systems was judged to be too major an undertaking, even with the advent of computer-assisted programming tools. Our only recourse was to scour the marketplace and buy an integrated management information system (MIS). Implicitly, this introduced a trade-off in our campus computing environment—accepting a generic, readily-available system and dispensing with the tradition of custom-designed, Dickinson-specific programming. This cannot be understated: the community must understand and embrace the reasoned stand that a vendor-supplied package cannot be customized to the extent that the old home-grown programs were.

BUILDING THE SHOPPING LIST

What were the campus-wide expectations for the new MIS package? How could we quantify them? How would the final choice be selected? Coincidentally, the structure of Dickinson's computing organization was completely revamped. An eleven-member administrative computing committee was established, chaired by the Assistant to the President, with appointments of the Computer Services managers and the heads of each major administrative department. This committee was instrumental in many ways during the MIS selection process, far beyond assisting with the many tasks that evolved. Ultimately, I truly believe the committee's involvement opened up the sense of ownership and responsibility for the project. Put bluntly, each member knew full well that the ultimate recommendation was made collectively and not by "them" (the Computer Center, senior management, etc.).

The committee first spent some budgeted dollars to bring a well-known consultant to campus to help us launch the search process. Over several days he interviewed the staff of every administrative department on campus, including Computer Services, to compile a report on inter-departmental data flow and an assessment of computing requirements. His visit and report gave us the spark to develop our first Request for Proposal (RFP).

THE SOFTWARE RFP

Given my experience with the college's administrative computing environment, I was appointed editor of the Request for Proposal (RFP). Each department compiled a list of expectations for the new MIS which I reviewed, sometimes expanded, and then reworked into a consistent format. The computing committee wanted to present potential vendors with a document that fully captured our expectations and that would, in turn, solicit unambiguous responses from the vendor. (We anticipated that the RFP, annotated with the vendor's responses, would become part of the final contract.) Eight months later, the final, comprehensive, consistent-looking document was compiled.

The first draft of Dickinson's software RFP comprised 106 pages! We had one section of common requirements, a section for every administrative department, and Computer Services. We chose the style where each requirement was a statement, often subdivided into very specific details. For example:

16. Ability of a utility for conducting ad hoc inquiries and report generation, where:
16.1. There are powerful functions including:
16.1.1. Math (e.g., sum, average, division, multiplication)
16.1.2. Multi-level sorts (e.g., by zip code, last name, first name)

We requested that bidders score each item on a scale of four to zero. The scale showed on each page as an italicized footer, explaining:

4 (currently in place); 3 (available with non-programming modification); 2 (available with programming modification); 1 (to be available in future release); 0 (not possible). These short responses should be further explained, in detail by the vendor.

This process got each department thinking about specific improvements in its computing environment. It involved a healthy self-examination of established office procedures. The process of generating the RFP also planted the seeds of change campus-wide.

PLAYERS ON THE HOME FIELD

Initially, Computer Services launched an informal market search for MIS packages utilizing Dickinson's existing computing environment. We were very familiar with the operating system and liked the utilities and the security it offered.

There were several packages available on this platform, and we decided to go for a deeper look. Three of us attended a spirited user group for one of these systems. This was our first glimpse at how vendors and system users got along. It was encouraging to see a genuine unity of purpose, and that folks on both ends of the support line could actually have fun together!

We invited that vendor to visit our campus for two days of in-depth demonstrations and question/answer sessions. Clerks, office managers, and directors from major administrative departments each had several hours to examine the software and question the vendor. Some of the College's senior staff met briefly with the vendor's bigwigs. Within five months, we put a second vendor through the same ringer at our campus.

The process was useful in several ways. The entire administrative community got involved, from clerks to senior staff. It brought the strengths and weaknesses of the product into focus, and eventually into our RFP. Afterwards, each vendor commented that the experience at Dickinson had been unusually grueling because of the range of questions and the high expectations voiced by the attenders.

After looking closely at these two packages, the reviews were mixed. Some modules were clearly superior and some were quite inferior to the home-grown systems in place. From a look under the hood, we concluded that the fundamental architecture would be limiting.

Two other vendors looked interesting, and we invited them to campus for our now standard two-day affair. One product was based on an up-and-coming database architecture, which our "techies" found exciting. We soon learned, however, the vendor had little software we could actually run, lots of "vaporware," and an uncomfortably small customer base. The other vendor had an established base of schools using its financial system but was still developing a student records component. Though some vendors hinted at lucrative offers to serve as beta test sites for their emerging systems, we declined. The computing committee stood united that we could not risk the success of the project or the business of the college.

To some, there was a letdown because an instant improvement was unavailable. To others, it was comforting that we would preserve the status quo a little longer.

PLAYERS ON A NEW FIELD

Realizing the limitations of the 1988 marketplace, we took a second look at developing our own systems. We visited two schools that were developing systems using fourth generation languages and CASE tools. But even though this atmosphere was inherently more productive than our traditional Cobol programming methods, the development cycle still would be too long and require more resources than we could muster.

After more than a year of looking, we were now out of viable software options for our existing computing environment. We would have to look to a new hardware platform as well. This was a major disappointment to Computer Services, as the complexity of the implementation project had just increased by an order of magnitude.

We quickly found two vendors offering a very similar product and an established customer base, though with uncomfortably foreign hardware and operating systems. Both vendors came to campus for a two-day inquisition, and the committee was actually impressed with one of the alternatives! At last the campus administrative staff found a software option that they thought had real possibilities.

OUTSIDE OPINIONS

Did we miss some critical area in our search strategy? How did our RFP documents measure up to industry standards? We only had one chance to select the software and hardware and really wanted some reassurance that we had covered all the bases.

Committee members scouted out the world of consultants, and invited two candidates to campus for interviews. Though the firms presented comprehensive services, from compiling the RFP to final contract negotiations, we were interested only in tapping their expertise at certain points during the selection process. We contracted the services of one well-known firm for a short time. The technical guidance we sought from them for a hardware benchmark test (below) was very disappointing. While reviewing our search process, the consultant offered a few good tips, though essentially he left us with the feeling that indeed we were on the right track. The committee was most comfortable proceeding in our own Dickinsonian way.

CLOSING IN ON THE SOFTWARE

We sent copies of our first RFP to three vendors. Two responded in detail, the third begged off (hard to rate vaporware, maybe?). During the RFP cycle, we made many visits and/or telephone calls to the vendors' headquarters.

Committee members contacted peers at institutions using the contending MIS packages. By and large, people genuinely seemed to enjoy discussing their computing systems. Through these conversations, our computing community learned more about these other systems in terms of functionality, vendor support, and hardware responsiveness. These insights helped shape our final RFP.

Feelers were also sent out by our institutional contacts on Wall Street about the financial strengths or weaknesses of each vendor's enterprise. This is as important an aspect today as it was in 1989, given the volatile nature of the computing industry.

The administrative computing committee briefed its academic counterpart. The faculty raised concerns about the cost to the institution of the MIS. We presented a summary of the search and responded to questions. The same group briefed the senior staff and the head of the board of trustees. We wanted to do the politically correct thing!

CLOSING IN ON THE HARDWARE

Given our expectations on system response time, we insisted on a benchmark test. We developed a scenario constituting a representative computing load at Dickinson, and asked the vendor to run it while we ran interactive tests. The first vendor's best machine was unsatisfactory to us. The response time reminded us of our own overworked minicomputer on a busy day! (While on the benchmark trip, we also visited a nearby school using contending software.) The next benchmark test was closer to home, but it was no more successful. We had the software pretty much picked out, but couldn't find a machine that would run it! This was a tremendous letdown, especially for the computing committee.

Fortunately, in very short order the software vendor ported its MIS to another machine. We did a third benchmark test, and this time things hummed. Quite honestly, by now we had been emotionally up and down too many times for celebration, but we certainly felt a quiet satisfaction that our search netted a true winner.

Another area of concern was precisely how data communications would be established. Dickinson has a PBX system supporting voice/data transmission from every desktop. Terminal servers pass data from the telephone system to minicomputers. The minicomputers are networked for high-speed data sharing. How would the new UNIX computer fit seamlessly into this mix? We hosted a gathering of experts from the hardware vendors, the PBX system and the leading software vendor. It was a curious meeting, but some good information was exchanged (though ultimately the communications solution was developed in-house).

We learned enough about the native operating system to know that certain third-party utilities would have to be purchased. We sought utilities producing periodic backup tapes, remote printer spooling, and enhanced security mechanisms. After going full-circle on the microcomputer- versus minicomputer-based word processing debate, we decided on the latter given the volume of correspondence emanating from MIS-based information.

Our 53-page hardware RFP addressed all of these elements and concerns. The format was similar to the software RFP mentioned above, except the bidder was asked to respond:

> "Y" operating system as supplied supports the requirement; "P" procedures must be written to meet the requirement; "T" third party software is required to meet the requirement; "N" the requirement cannot be met. All responses other than "Y" should include an explanatory comment."

These were major concerns for Computer Services, for what good is a new MIS if you can't access it? These issues were too technical for the rest of the committee to help negotiate, but were a source of high anxiety for us.

BUDGET

The committee and Computer Services established the elements of the project that would require funding and collected initial quotations from vendors. When identifying hardware costs, we considered the central computer and peripherals, desktop devices to provide adequate system access, remote printers for local printing from the MIS, facilities upgrades for the new equipment (air conditioning? power? floor space?), communications, and maintenance.

For software, besides the licensing costs of the MIS itself, we projected funds needed for acquiring source code, training in the operating system, training in the MIS (on-site options are sometimes more cost-effective), on-site consulting days from the software vendor and annual maintenance costs.

Personnel costs proved to be tricky to predict. (We review the new staffing requirements, below.) On our campus, we experienced a sharp rise in overtime costs as departmental staff worked with the development group during the conversion phase, and again later during final testing prior to implementation. The preferred alternative, "comp time," was not feasible; nobody could afford to take any time off! We had not projected an allowance for overtime pay.

From discussions with peers at other institutions and with the vendor, we developed the expectation that regular attendance at user groups was essential both for users and Computer Services. This forum is extremely worthwhile in terms of knowledge gained and contacts made. These contacts can be a very useful resource when solving problems. Collectively, these voices are heard clearly by the vendor. Plus, user groups can be fun! We budget annually for the cost of attending user groups.

A DONE DEAL

The final software and hardware RFPs were sent to the vendors. The Treasurer conducted the actual contract negotiations. Eventually a deal was struck, some two years after our first informal foray into the marketplace. As we turned toward the future, a sigh of relief was heard across the campus!

NEW STAFF—THE GOAL

We made the case that this wholesale replacement of the entrenched administrative computing environment would require additional personnel. We anticipated that it would be a major effort to install the base system and to make the significant amount of programming customizations, let alone the parallel workload of maintaining an adequate level of service for the established administrative computing responsibilities. Many staffing models were considered, including those offered by our software vendor. A systems development group was hired, consisting of a manager and two programmer/analysts. The manager and I are peers, reporting to the Director of Computer Services. A documenter/trainer position and a part-time secretary were added to my support staff.

The interaction between the development group and my traditional support group was a major concern. I envisioned things would work something like a relay race. My group could help the implementation team by providing a historical perspective of tasks and values, by extracting data from the old systems for use by conversion programs, and by keeping the rest of the administrative computing functions humming along. Once a module went live, the baton of support would be passed back to us, so the implementation team could move on to the next module. That was the theory.

NEW STAFF—THE REALITY

In practice, the blend of newcomers and traditionalists has been surprisingly successful. Key elements for our success seem to be a positive "can-do" attitude, team spirit, open communication, a formal task log, a weekly meeting to review the open tasks, and a sometimes tricky compromise between historical standards and the reality of the time crunch inherent in any implementation. As the leader of a group of traditionalists, I can say this created some rough moments during the implementation.

It takes a real effort to convert data from established systems to the purchased MIS. This process pits the styles of the new group and the traditionalists face-to-face, and it isn't always smooth. Mapping the data from one system to another is extremely tedious, especially as the implementation and the other administrative computing responsibilities relentlessly continue. But through this process, the old-timers really can help maximize the automated transfer of time-tested data, and certainly can learn much about the new MIS. The implementation group gains valuable insights into the scope of existing functionality, and learns something of the value of the traditional methodology.

TASK LOG

Early on, we established a formal task log system in which every request for support, programming, and product development is captured. We didn't want anything to "fall through the cracks!" Each request is tracked by module, category (programming, documentation, etc.) and method (e-mail, telephone, etc.). When a task is completed, the solution is entered into the database. The result is a valuable reference for future problem solving and a source for monitoring activity. Perhaps most important, this system provides a ready-made agenda for the weekly meetings between me and my systems development counterpart. We review the status of the "hot" items and can look ahead to those on the horizon. Recently, we've begun distributing the open task log to module representatives at campus user group meetings.

DEVELOPMENT METHODOLOGY

The primary objective for a consistent development methodology is to maximize efficiency and support. For example, through file- and directory-naming conventions, the programmer can most quickly locate the source code for a program under scrutiny. Subroutines named meaningfully and stored in a specific directory structure can be quickly located and retrieved (rather than overlooked and redeveloped from scratch).

We're now stepping back to address good programming standards and development methodologies. While this may seem backwards, it represents one of the compromises to which I previously alluded. By the time the new team came on board, the clock was ticking furiously and the implementation had to move full-speed ahead. The lack of formal methodologies sometimes did cause problems for the production group and the end user but, again, through good communication and cooperation, those problems usually were ironed out in short order.

One procedure that helps immensely is a formal acceptance sheet, whereby the end user and/or my support group tests and then accepts in writing the custom program or modification. We do not remove a programming request from the task log until this acceptance form has been completed.

DOCUMENTATION/TRAINING

We anticipated the need for a new, full-time employee to present the computing community with MIS training and to prepare site-specific documentation. As a module was going live, the trainer offered classes to familiarize the users with concepts of the integrated MIS, the jargon, and some of the features. A five-part class on the ad hoc inquiry and reporting language was also developed. We felt that a Dickinson employee would be more approachable and accessible than an outsider, thereby reducing anxiety and promoting a smoother implementation. Also, we sought to avoid the time and expense of sending the administrative community to generic vendor-supplied training. We saw the need for custom documentation to explain how Dickinson uses each module, especially given our extensive programming modifications, as a supplement to the vendor-supplied manuals.

In reality, for most of the first year the trainer's time was consumed in directly assisting with the implementation. This was part of the compromise, too. There were simply too many issues afoot for the implementation team to address simultaneously. But now the implementation has progressed to the point that my support group can handle most of the help calls, and the documenter/trainer can focus on her primary responsibilities.

Interestingly, "documentation" has taken many forms beyond the module-specific manuals. It includes processing checklists, yearly data processing schedules pointing to those checklists, quick-reference guides (cheat sheets), a task log, and the name and address conventions.

OUT IN THE COMMUNITY

We had a few things going for us during the implementation phase at Dickinson. The staff of each department had already seen the software during the sales cycle. Many had talked to counterparts at other institutions using the package. During the RFP experience, each department focused its expectations for the new system. Some received vendor-supplied module training. All received some on-site training. Put simply, people knew what was coming in the new MIS.

Pardon the generality, but while change is normal for the staff of Computer Services, elsewhere in the computing community it seems that change introduces real anxiety, discomfort, and stress. Even though computers are no longer a novelty, to many they remain a source of fear. With the implementation of new software came new hardware, so nothing about the computing environment was the same as before. With nearly every module, at one point or another, these human emotions affected the atmosphere of the implementation.

As for the new MIS itself, it definitely evoked strong feelings in the administrative community! Some felt the features and capabilities of the new system required too much maintenance. In some applications, the new MIS was more labor-intensive than its home-grown predecessor. Not everyone was pleased with the new world. On the other hand, many applications were enthusiastically received, and custom programming helped to fill the voids.

THE CAMPUS USER GROUP

During the implementation phase, those with hands-on experience—data entry clerks and office managers—got involved. This is easier said than done, since everyone already has a full-time job! To preserve and promote this level of participation beyond the implementation, a hands-on user group was created. This committee consists of a representative from each major administrative department, the two computing coordinators, and the documenter/trainer.

Officially, the committee resolves detailed problems involved with sharing data in the integrated system. One shining example is the set of name and address conventions, listing the data entry standards for names and addresses and defining which office maintains each address type. Equally important, the MIS novices get comfort and support from the more experienced system users in the friendly atmosphere of committee meetings.

IN OUR OWN HOUSE

In Computer Services, certain aspects of the implementation have been unpleasant. The traditionalists think we've lost a bit of the control we once held. I don't mean for that to sound authoritarian: we knew our home-grown Cobol software inside and out. If a change was requested, we knew instantly whether it was doable. The operating system had a pretty friendly command line language, and there was no database management layer of software to traverse. No development group with which to coordinate efforts existed. Now we have to share the spotlight!

With the new MIS, when we're asked a first-time question, we usually have to do some research before offering an answer. The task log helps us keep track of these questions. Typically we pore over documentation, simulate the problem in the test area, quiz the development group, and sometimes wait for a reply from the vendor's support line. We can't offer the instant answer like we used to, and that annoys us.

Some problems are very elusive. Does the program have a bug? Is there a problem with the database management package? Is the problem at the operating system level? We've had a difficult time ironing out data transfers across applications when the operating system protection scheme comes into play.

Even the operating system (a derivative of UNIX) is new territory. Boy do we miss the batch queues and full-screen text editor in our previous environment!

DATA SECURITY AND RESPONSIBILITY

The strength of the integrated system lies in the inherent accessibility to common sets of data. But from the aspect of security, access to shared data is a fundamental weakness!

The administrative computing committee asked Computer Services to produce a formal security document outlining the proper use of MIS data, and a hierarchy of responsibility for data in each module. This plan was formally adopted after a great deal of input by the administrative users. Through the plan, we hope to provide a lasting framework against which data access can be judged. Through a statement of understanding, we hope to provide a reminder about the responsibilities involved with accessing, reporting, and handling confidential data. Every member of the administrative computing community has signed that statement of understanding.

Quite frankly, the issue of data access and security has consumed tremendous energy at our campus. Even now, after we've been live for two full years on some modules, and after discussing and developing the data security plan, this is still a major concern. Even in the face of a significant programming backlog, we may need to build additional barriers against possible security breaches.

CLEAN-UP PHASE

Some veterans of implementations warned us that once a module went live, there would follow a period devoted to tedious and mundane chores—minor program modifications or screen changes, new programs to generate supplemental reports, general clean-up from data conversions, etc. It's all true! It's not glamorous, but it's essential.

CONCLUSIONS

We're committed to making our new management information system work the way our campus community wants it to work. We're very picky. What we've selected isn't perfect, but we still think it is the best available, affordable, functional option. Despite the intricate implementation process and the human emotions involved, it's significant that since the first module, payroll, came up back in January 1991, we've never missed a pay date, never gotten the checks out late. Despite the anxiety along the way, by and large the system is working for us.

We're in a new world but we're not alone. Through committee structures or in casual conversations, members of the administrative computing community seem to be communicating like never before. We made it through the implementation together! At MIS user groups or across the Internet, while we seek out the wizened veterans, newcomers are starting to ask us questions!

Our methodologies and efforts have paid off in a successful implementation. Yet despite all the preparation, I never fully anticipated the very real human emotions involved—channeled effectively they help avoid failure and help guarantee success. That is my incentive to share this account of the people and processes in our successful odyssey from home-grown systems to a commercial MIS package.

CHAPTER FIVE

THE ADMINISTRATIVE SOFTWARE EVALUATION COMMITTEE

Dagrun Bennett
Director of Computer Services
Franklin College

The thought of changing administrative software is daunting at best, and the more automated the administrative process already is, the more frightening it becomes to think about a total conversion of the existing system. Computers and software affect the way people work in fundamental ways, and unless change is perceived to mean improvement, it is not welcome. We are all familiar with the stubborn resistance that can undermine good projects because key people feel excluded from the planning and decision process. It matters not how good a decision may be if it is imposed on people whose daily work environment and ability to perform their jobs will be altered; such a decision will be viewed with suspicion. For a change to be successful, people at all levels of the organization need to feel involved, their ideas must be heard, and they must accept responsibility for the project.

Many theories and strategies are available to guide the process of software selection and implementation—top-down, bottom up, and structured, to mention but a few—but in the end it comes down to finding a way for people with different needs to define those needs, modify them when necessary, redefine and compromise, and then agree to a solution that benefits everyone. When Franklin College was faced with the challenge of improving administrative reporting and record keeping capabilities, a carefully selected committee took ownership of the project and developed a method of cooperative group decision making that has guided the implementation as well as the selection process.

Franklin College is a traditional liberal arts college with 900 students. Although we like to think of ourselves as unique, we are probably no more so than other small liberal arts schools except for the defining events of the "fire years." In the spring of 1985, we had two major fires; first a dormitory burned to the ground, and three and a half weeks later the main administration building was severely damaged. Everyone who had worked in "Old Main" spent the next two years in temporary quarters: the president borrowed the chaplain's office; the dean shared a lounge with the registrar and records office staff; faculty were everywhere from the meditation room to construction trailers in the parking lot. Classes were taught in the snack-bar and former storage rooms. The computer center took over a study lounge and two small classrooms in the library. Life was disrupted and inconvenient for everyone, but what could have been the beginning of the end for a small struggling college became a unifying new beginning. This campus displays a sense of common purpose, of pride in what has been accomplished, and recognition that it could only have been done through cooperation and commitment to a common goal.

Within days of the fires, the development office started planning a massive campaign to raise money for rebuilding, thus placing very heavy demands on the six-year-old computer and our mostly in-house developed software. All the other offices experienced a similar increase in demands, and at the same time academic computing needs were growing rapidly. But with the overwhelming demands the construction activity placed on the institution's resources, for the next two years the computer center staff could only cope to the best of its ability, and dream and plan.

When the rebuilding was done, the computer center moved into new facilities in the administration building with two instructional laboratories, good office space and, for the first time in its history, a proper computer room. All the new equipment and software put enormous demands on the computer center staff of three. By the fall of 1989, the college was finally in a position to evaluate its administrative software options, and the Administrative Software Evaluation Committee (ASEC) was born.

The ASEC members were chosen with care. The committee needed the support of the top administrators because its recommendations would require a long-term commitment of college resources. Its work had to be given high priority because committee members would be required to spend a great deal of time on the tasks assigned to them, and the quality of their decisions would determine how well the college could implement the vision for the future as conceived by the board of trustees. After much deliberation, it was decided that the management level below vice president would be the most appropriate. These managers know the type of information and reports the officers of the college need, but they are also intimately involved with the data that produces these reports. They know how the data is collected and understand the requirements of the office staff.

The ASEC convened in September, 1989. It was chaired by the director of the computer center, and included the administrative systems analyst (a new position in the computer center) and a representative from each functional area:

the associate director of admissions and financial aid, the business office controller, the director of development services, the registrar, and the director of student life. The committee was charged with providing all the administrative offices at Franklin College with the computing capabilities needed to perform effectively as we headed into the 1990s. This was to be accomplished in a manner as timely and cost-effective as possible while keeping to the guidelines established in the college's Information Technology Policy.

At the first meeting three options were identified: (1) refinement and continued development of the existing software, (2) in-house development of new applications based on relational database technology, and (3) purchase of a commercially developed software package. The first and second options would give applications that were tailored to the institution's idiosyncrasies, but the committee unanimously turned them both down. The magnitude of the project and the size of the computer center staff dictated a search for a vendor that could provide an existing software solution. The committee planned to make a recommendation to the president's cabinet in March 1990. This would allow time for the proposal to be presented to the college's board of trustees at their April, 1990 meeting.

The selection process followed the standard guidelines for systems analysis. In biweekly meetings the committee established criteria and developed evaluation tools. Each office provided its own specific requirements, and each software system that passed the initial screening was rated against these requirements. Computer center staff guided the process, asking questions and making suggestions, but it was always clearly understood that the committee members were responsible for defining all functional requirements for their areas. For the software that met the specifications that had been established by the committee, each member of ASEC contacted his or her counterparts at colleges that were using the software, and reported their findings back to the committee. There was no package that met all the specifications of all the offices, but since it was important to the group to find software that would provide a truly integrated system, each administrative area sacrificed some functionality in order to agree on one solution. Throughout the selection process the committee's understanding of the need to compromise and cooperate was truly remarkable.

On March 12, 1990, the committee made a recommendation to the president's cabinet to purchase a commercially developed software package that would provide an integrated solution to administrative software needs. The software was to be implemented in planned stages, and would require additional hardware before all of the offices could be included. The college signed a contract with the vendor in April, 1990.

The ASEC's work was so outstanding that the president asked the committee to continue as a working group during the conversion and implementation phase. In addition to the original members, the director of development research and the director of financial aid joined the group. Planning the migration to the new software started immediately, and over the next two years the college information system was converted, new features were implemented, and the necessary customizations were identified and prioritized.

The committee met at least once a month to discuss progress or the lack of it. Computer center staff brought up policy issues and other concerns of common interest. Everyone was encouraged to discuss the problems they had encountered; someone else might already have solved them. Since a problem could be common to all areas or unique to only one office, the quickest way to find out was through open discussion by the whole group. The meetings also provided an opportunity to monitor where different offices were in the process of conversion. Everything within the college was interrelated, and the success of one project depended on the completion of another. When an office fell behind schedule, it had a ripple effect. The ASEC meetings showed everyone the extent of this interdependence, and put pressure on the struggling office to get back on schedule.

Each semester, ASEC developed a time line of events and deadlines: identifying tasks, completion dates, and the office responsible for performing the assignment. The greatest frustrations surfaced in allocating computer center staff time and in prioritizing needs for customizations. However, the committee worked out a way of giving an office primary access to computer center staff at certain times, taking turns according to the stages of implementation. Each office ranked its needs for customization, and the priorities were negotiated.

Besides solving problems of timing, consistency, formats, and conventions, ASEC members communicated the status of the different projects to their vice presidents and their office personnel. Having one person in each area serve as the focal point of information distribution helped to maintain consistency and minimized confusion and misinformation.

As the conversion progressed it became clear that consistency in procedures, timing, and data needed constant attention. At this point ASEC produced a spin-off: the College Wide Information Consistency Committee (CWICC). ASEC members often attended the monthly CWICC meetings, but the latter group consisted primarily of support staff. The increased communication between the people "in the trenches" helped us avoid many pitfalls, and formed an invaluable support group for new users. When an office started implementing the new software and converting data from the old system, the staff had access to people who could guide them around obstacles they had run into themselves, and give them the myriad of hints and suggestions that only experience provides.

It became clear early in the conversion that the planned hardware upgrade would be needed sooner than projected in the original proposal. ASEC prepared a status report for the president's cabinet, recommending a substantial investment in hardware. Since the committee represented all administrative areas and individual members had kept their vice presidents informed throughout the conversion process, the groundwork had been laid. When a decision was not made quickly enough, ASEC members found opportunities to remind their vice presidents that this was not for the benefit of one area at the expense of another, but a common need that had to be met. Once again the group's sense of unity proved to be a convincing argument, and the cabinet approved the purchase of new hardware.

In several instances a concern voiced in an ASEC meeting became a group project. The enthusiasm and energy generated by free and easy exchange of ideas sometimes seemed to move mountains. For example, there was no user group connected with the vendor. As the conversion progressed, it became clear that it would be of real benefit to all our staff to be able to communicate with and learn from users at other institutions. ASEC decided to start a user group and hold a conference at Franklin College. It took six months to secure the cooperation of the vendor, organize the group, recruit speakers and arrange the details. The first conference was attended by seventy people from all over the country, and has been followed by regularly scheduled meetings hosted by other colleges. Franklin College users now have a support network. This user group facilitates the relationship with the vendor by providing a common voice, and helps set priorities for the development of new features.

Halfway through the conversion, Franklin College secured a foundation grant to fund a two-year position in administrative computing to assist the software migration. These grants had never before been given for administrative software conversions. One of the main reasons for selecting Franklin College was the foundation's interest in the ASEC's unique approach to decision making and problem resolution. By encouraging input from all administrative offices and involving them in the process, the college has not only reaped the benefits of the approach, but has also gained recognition and outside funding to continue the process.

The strong sense of unity of purpose has had another interesting effect. Originally charged with the evaluation and selection of administrative software, the committee was redefined for the first time when the president requested it to guide the conversion and implementation. Throughout the project stages, the committee has adapted itself to the changing needs of the process. Implementation is almost complete now, and one recent ASEC meeting was devoted to a discussion of the committee's future. Its members agreed that new needs identified can best be met through the active cooperation of this strategically placed group, and it has redefined itself, with a new mission statement, objectives, and goals.

High on the list of objectives is maintaining an interactive relationship with the vendor. The viability of the software becomes increasingly important as the college becomes more dependent on it. At the same time both the climate in higher education and the increasing sophistication of the administrative users demand a high degree of flexibility. ASEC members are therefore concerned about being able to comment on the vendor's future direction and product development. The relationship with the vendor is seen as a partnership, with Franklin College fulfilling its obligations by providing feedback on current features and information about necessary enhancements.

Computer center directors serve on many committees. Some committees are amiable but inefficient, and accomplish very little. Some are many-headed monsters; they also accomplish very little. The ASEC has been unique. Clearly there are many reasons for this. All members have a great deal at stake in making the process work. Their ability to perform their jobs depends fully on the committee's decisions. They have hands-on experience with all the large and small issues about which they make decisions. They are at an organizational level where they understand those decisions' effects both on the people who use the information and those who produce it. In the implementation phase, ASEC members were always aware that they had been part of the selection team; this was a powerful incentive to finding solutions to the problems that are an inevitable part of any conversion.

But there seems to be something else at work as well: a phenomenon that flies in the face of all professional systems training. Systems analysts all know that a large and complex problem requires the appointment of a project leader and then the breaking down of the problem into manageable pieces to be solved one by one. Presto! the complex system works. Systems analysts also know that reality does not conform smoothly to this theory. Emerging from the experience at Franklin College is the realization that in exposing a group of people to the full complexity of their joint undertaking, those people approach the solution to their own part of the puzzle with a different mind-set. Each one knows that other parts are equally as difficult, and that a solution occurs only if it works for everybody. The process is not one of constant harmony and bliss—individual members often feel frustrated. But throughout the long and difficult process, ASEC has continued to function as a group, and the group has made decisions that are much more farsighted than any member could have made alone.

Chapter Six

UPGRADING ADMINISTRATIVE COMPUTING FOR FREE: THE MIRACLE OF RAPID TECHNOLOGICAL ADVANCE

Lou Miller
Director, Computer Services
Rollins College

In the Spring of 1992 Rollins College realized that its eight-year-old Microdata administrative minicomputer was no longer capable of meeting the growing demands placed upon it, and that replacing the system could no longer be postponed. While nearly everyone on campus agreed that the computer needed to be upgraded, there was vital concern about financing. In a period of nationwide economic recession and with an increasing struggle to maintain enrollments, any significant capital outlay had to be considered carefully. With some pessimism about the probable outcome of the investigation, Computer Services undertook an exploration of options and costs. What was found, as described below, is that the advance of technology had created a near miraculous circumstance—one that is of certain interest to any institution in a similar situation. We discovered that the administrative computer could be significantly upgraded for no more than the cost of maintaining and operating the old system.

THE OLD ADMINISTRATIVE SYSTEM

The administrative computer on hand was a Microdata 9230 with three megabytes of RAM, 520 megabytes of hard disk storage, and a 1600/3200-bpi, 9-track, 1/2-inch magnetic tape unit. The 9230 had a MIC performance rating of approximately seven. The system had 128 asynchronous ports connected to printers and terminals, or microcomputers running terminal emulation software, located throughout the campus and at three remote locations. Almost all of the campus connections were direct wired with individual cables running to each connected device on campus.

The primary application software was a Pick operating system called "REALITY." Because of its age, the computer system could run only Version

53

5.2 of REALITY even though Version 7.0 had been released for newer equipment. The incapability to run current versions of the operating system was one of the compelling reasons for wanting to upgrade. The system had a programming language—Data/Basic, an inquiry language—ENGLISH, and a command language—PROC. All were used to maintain the administrative relational database that contains student records, faculty and staff information, alumni and development data, and all campus financial and accounting information. The Rollins MIS program library was originally developed by CAMPUS/Reality in 1976, but had been extensively modified by our programming staff since then. The staff had written nearly two thousand programs, customized to each department's request and accessible through a comprehensive menu system.

UPGRADE BUDGET

While sympathetic to the need to upgrade administrative computing, the senior administration did not believe the college could incur additional debt during the current recessionary period. They did agree, however, to let Computer Services pursue any improvements that could be accomplished within the existing expenditure levels. Because the Microdata was purchased eight years ago, the purchase debt had been retired. The hardware and software maintenance agreements, however, cost $2,700 a month. Because the initial plan was to lease a system for a five-year period, the five-year cost of the existing system was calculated, including a 5 percent projected annual rate maintenance contracts increases, at $179,000.

In addition to maintenance contracts, one additional factor was considered in calculating the operating costs of the old system. Preliminary investigations revealed that new systems with the performance we were seeking typically consume less than a tenth of the electricity of the Microdata 9230. Based on local electrical charges, we estimated savings of approximately $2,100 per year in energy costs, or $10,500 over the five-year period. Thus, the budget for the upgrade became $189,500. If the Microdata could be replaced by a newer and more powerful system within budget, it could be said that the upgrade was free.

UPGRADE GOALS

After ascertaining the funding limits, the next step was to define the requirements for any new system. We decided that the primary goal was not to obtain significant improvement in processing power, but to move to more standard hardware and software. Any increase in speed of operation would be welcome, but only in the very busiest periods at the end of the academic year did response times for users on the 9230 become noticeably slow. On numerous occasions, however, users and the programmers had returned from conferences wanting to explore the possibility of adopting exciting new software they had seen demonstrated. Almost invariably, they discovered that the packages were not compatible with our configuration. Therefore, we were highly desirous of moving into the mainstream of computing hardware and software.

A second major objective was to provide better communications. The number of ports had been expanded to the maximum supported by the existing hardware, but numerous demands existed for more ports. Several offices had resorted to the less than desirable expedient of having multiple terminals connected to a single port with switch boxes allowing any one terminal to be active. Rather than seeking to increase the number of asynchronous connections, we decided to move towards more modern networking communications. In part, the intent was to obtain faster transmission speeds to better support file transfers and windowed interfaces. Of perhaps even greater concern was the desire to use optical fiber as a transmission medium because Rollins is located in an area of extremely high lightning activity. A final communications concern was to develop TCP/IP connectivity to other minicomputers on campus including the academic VAX, the business services' Hewlett Packard computer, and the library's PDP-based system.

Several somewhat lower order objectives were also established. More disk storage space was needed to respond to increasing demands to keep more data online. Many offices needed to access older data either for newly mandated government reports, or to be better able to track past performance so as to improve planning. The Microdata system operators, who would also operate the new system, let it be known they would be more productive, and especially thankful, if a backup device could be obtained with enough capacity that they did not have to change tape reels several times during a backup. Another concern was that the Microdata system did not have an uninterruptible power supply. In an area subject to frequent power outages, having a UPS seemed essential. Finally, there was a need to improve our hardware and software maintenance coverage. The existing contract provided service from 8:00 am to 5:00 pm Monday through Friday. The terms of the agreement meant that in order to effect repairs, system users had to be denied access during working hours. Because so many offices had become so dependent upon the system, it was believed that a 7-day, 24-hour agreement would be less disruptive of essential work.

COMPATIBILITY OBJECTIVES

While the need to upgrade and move to more standard software was clear, there was concern that the extensive programming and learning efforts over the years not be lost. Therefore, in addition to the upgrade goals, objectives concerning the compatibility of any new system to the existing system were formulated. We had written a comprehensive set of custom, menu-driven programs for every department on campus. There was no user pressure to move to one of the standard university administrative software packages, and we could not have afforded it even if there had been such demand. Therefore, it was deemed essential either that existing programs should work on any new system, or that the conversion of the programs to work on the new equipment be part of the upgrade. Because one of the major objectives was to move to a more standard software, it seemed likely that a conversion house would have to be employed to convert existing programs.

A second concern was to provide the training necessary for our programming staff and operations staff. The objective was to obtain a Pick-like database package that would allow the programmers to use their existing programming knowledge to be productive immediately under the new system, but what was wanted would amount to a superset of the existing software's programming capabilities and a training program for all of the programmers would be essential to take advantage of any new capabilities. We were willing to accept a more radical change in operating systems than in the database programming environment. Such a change, however, would require more extensive retraining of our operators than was anticipated for our programmers.

A third concern was that while we planned to begin a move toward networked communications, the new system would have to support all existing asynchronous communication lines. We had strong doubts that we could achieve other upgrade objectives within the budget, and we were convinced that it was not affordable to also network the campus. It might be three to five years before funding could be obtained for much networking outside the Computer Center itself. In the interim, it would be essential for any new computer to support the existing 128 asynchronous lines.

THE NEW ADMINISTRATIVE SYSTEM

Having established the upgrade and compatibility goals, we set about to determine what could be obtained within our budgetary restrictions. After reviewing several alternatives, an IBM RISC 6000 model 530H was chosen as the hardware for the upgrade. It has 64 megabytes of RAM, 2.4 gigabytes of disk space, a CD-ROM drive, a 525-megabyte, 1/4-inch cartridge tape drive, an external 9-track, 1600/3200-bpi, 1/2-inch tape drive, and, to the delight of the system operators, a 2.3-gigabyte, 8 mm tape drive for system backups. In addition to the requisite 128 asynchronous ports, the IBM has an Ethernet adapter. IBM provides a 24-hour, 7-day maintenance agreement, and the system includes a UPS.

The operating system for the RISC 6000 is AIX, IBM's version of UNIX. We chose the UNIVERSE DBMS to replace our REALITY database on the IBM. UNIVERSE is probably the most commonly used of the Pick-like database systems, permitting a relatively simple conversion of our existing programs and requiring minimal training for our programmers. APT Associates, a software conversion house, was retained to modify existing programs to run on the new system. Training in both AIX and UNIVERSE for our programmers and additional AIX training for our operators was also purchased.

A thin-wire TCP/IP network was established within the Computer Center by purchasing Ethernet adapters for each of our PCs and connecting them to the RISC 6000. NCSA Telnet was acquired for use as terminal emulation software. It has the significant advantage of being free to universities, and has the additional advantage of permitting concurrent connectivity to Computer Service's Novell server. The programmers are particularly pleased because they can open multiple sessions on the IBM, something they could not do on the Microdata.

COSTS

The IBM-based system described above met all of the goals and objectives, and showed a very substantial improvement in performance over the old Microdata. At question, however, is whether the cost of the upgrade was within budget. Were we able to upgrade so substantially for free? The hardware costs, including installation, were $59,222. The price for the AIX operating system software and the Universe DBMS was $47,622. It cost an additional $19,500 to have existing data and programs converted to run under UNIVERSE. Finally, $9,000 was spent to provide training for the programmers and operators. Summing the figures above, the entire system cost $135,344. In addition, maintenance contract costs are estimated to total $45,353 over a five-year period. The total cost of the upgrade, then, including hardware, software, conversion, training, and five years of maintenance agreements is $180,696. While this would appear to be $8,804 under budget, it ignores an important consideration.

Unfortunately, while the maintenance contracts would be spread over the five-year accounting period, the several suppliers of equipment, software, and services expected immediate payment of the $135,344 sum. The amount had to be borrowed and the interest costs added to our upgrade total. Over a five-year period, the interest will add $16,437 for a total five-year system upgrade cost of $197,134. We were $7,634 over budget. Had we failed to upgrade for free? Fortunately, another opportunity to save substantial sums by additional upgrades appeared.

ADDITIONAL SAVINGS

Having Ethernet capability on the new IBM led to an opportunity for savings in the cost of data communications between our administrative system and off-campus sites. Rollins has two buildings located within a half-mile of the main campus. The buildings have 31 PCs emulating data terminals and connected to the IBM computer via individual leased telephone lines. In September, the local telephone company doubled the monthly line charge, and announced a planned increase for next year which would raise costs to nearly triple the original rate. Even assuming no additional rate increases or additional lines, we estimated that the five-year cost for the communication lines would be in excess of $100,000.

Recently, Novell LANs had been established in both buildings and included all the microcomputers with leased line connections. It is planned to replace the individual data lines with a radio-based LAN bridge technology marketed by Persoft. The system is effective up to three miles given a reasonably clear line of sight, and it transfers two megabits of data per second. This data transfer rate is substantially greater than provided by the 9600 baud leased lines. A further advantage of the bridge alternative is that it met demands from both sites to connect additional users to the administrative system. All of the users connected to the LANs at the remote sites can have access to the administrative IBM, and new users can be added at the relatively low cost of a network interface card and cable. This communications solution not only provides substantially faster transmission, and connects more users, it proved substantially cheaper.

The purchase price of the hardware and software to connect our two buildings is $22,083. Adding the cost of a maintenance contract, $2,995 annually, would bring the five-year cost of the system to $34,063, a savings of more than $66,000 compared to leased lines. Clearly, these additional communications savings far more than offset the $7,634 that the upgrade exceeded budget. Not only can it be claimed that the upgrade was free, there is a reasonable basis to assert that it actually saved Rollins money.

SUMMARY

In the Spring of 1992, the Computer Services department of Rollins College set out to upgrade its administrative computer system under what appeared to be the stringent budget constraint that the total cost could not exceed what was currently being spent just to operate the existing system. Surprisingly, and delightfully, it was found that technological advances have not only substantially increased the capabilities of computer-related equipment, they have as dramatically decreased the cost of that hardware. We were able to meet all of our (not inconsequential) upgrade goals for less than it cost to keep our eight-year-old computer hardware and software. Other universities should be alert to the possibility that this miracle of modern technology may mean that they, like Rollins, can upgrade administrative computing for free!

CHAPTER SEVEN

A RADICAL APPROACH TO DATA NETWORKING

John Beckett
Director of Information Services
Southern College of Seventh-day Adventists

INTRODUCTION

Of course, you want a network. There are so many important things you can do with a network. That is why you are reading this book. It may be why your boss told you to read this book. Go ahead—develop your network. But don't wait for the multimillion-dollar, blue-sky plan to deliver useful products to prospective clients. Investigate every "reason" you have to build a network to see whether you can actually provide network-like services before the network actually arrives.

Case in point: access to student information. Our academic departments wanted the ability to "pull a student up on the screen," to see basic information about that student and on class schedules. They viewed departments in our administration—how we could just push a button and get answers so quickly—with envy!

Our administrators, however, were less than enthusiastic about connecting terminals all over campus to the central computer. After all, that computer contains the family jewels (transcripts and A/R information) and it is well known that hackers lurk out there. We felt that the best way to make mainframe information available to outlying offices was to copy it to a network server and let them read all they want. No problem if somebody messes up the data—it'll be rewritten with the next update. We had used this scenario for years between our administrative and academic computers, before the academicians abandoned timesharing for microcomputers.

Our problem was that we had no network. We had no staff position for developing and managing a network. No steam tunnels or conduit system to run fiber or coax through. No perception on our campus that a network was a resource we should pour money or effort into.

The solution was SCOOP, an acronym for Southern College Online Office Program. This combination of a database and access program makes it look to all PC users like they are online with our central database: no network; no online connection; just a bit of hard disk space. Updates are distributed at strategic points on the calendar, by floppy disk. Simple in concept, and inexpensive to implement, SCOOP is also an important first step in establishing how we will go about doing networking.

The first step in our design was to consider what information would be made available. At this point, we were not concerned about the distribution method. After much negotiating between departmental requests and the Records office, we classified all student data in one of three categories:

1. Directory Information. FERPA, the Federal Educational Rights to Privacy Act, also known as the "Buckley Amendment," allows a college to distribute certain information to anyone provided a student has not asked to be omitted from directories. For us this includes the student name, her/his "preferred name" (name used for informal address, often but not always her/his first name), local address and telephone number, sex, degree sought, major(s), minor(s), class standing (Freshman, Sophomore . . .), birthday (month/day, not year), parents' address, and student's professional objective. We further defined this information as pertaining to all students enrolled in the current semester, the previous two semesters, or accepted for the coming semester.

2. General Administrative. A larger group of information includes directory data plus items that may be viewed by any employee of the college who is involved in student administration. The data description for this group includes the list above, plus the advisor's name, parents' names and telephone numbers, the student's high school, campus ID number (we do not use SSN for a primary ID), and lists of classes for the current and previous two semesters.

3. Office Restricted. Any data not included above is made available only on a specific need-to-know basis. We decided that this category of data would not be distributed to computers across campus. We decided to focus on the "General Administrative" category for our project. The data to be included is detailed below.

DATABASE DESIGN

We designed the database using dBase III-Plus structures. It was felt that this format would give us compatibility with more software and more future uses than anything else. Three data files are included: STUDENT, STUCLAS, and CLASS (Figure 7.1). The first has one record per student. The second has one record for each class that each student is taking. The third has one record per class.

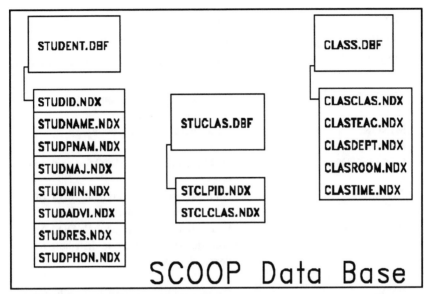

Figure 7.1 Data File Relationship

For each student there is a record in the STUDENT file with the following items:

PID	Pseudo-ID. A 5-digit numeric identifier used primarily as the student's key in the Student/Class file.
NAME	Student name, formatted last name first, followed by a comma and space, then first name, then middle name.
PREFNAME	Student's "preferred" name. Most often a first name, but may be a nickname or a middle name.
SADR1	Student's campus address. Line 1 is usually empty.
SADR2	
SCITY	
SSTATE	
SZIP	
RESIDENCE	A 4-character code convenient for identifying dormitory and room. When sending out a mailing to dorm students, we will use this as a sort key.
TELEPHONE	Student's local telephone number.

SEX	"M " or "F "
DEGREE	Type of degree sought: BS, BA, AS, etc.
MAJOR	Four-character major code: MATH, PSYC, etc.
MAJOR2	Second major (only once have we had more than two majors).
MINOR	Four-character minor code.
MINOR2	
CLASSSTDG	"FR" for Freshman, "SO" for Sophomore, etc.
ADVISOR	Name of student's advisor. Most of our faculty members have advisees.
BIRTHDAY	Four characters, coded MMDD. Age is considered too private to distribute to academic departments.
PARENTNAME	
PADR1	Parents' address. Line 1 is usually empty
PADR2	
PCITY	
PSTATE	
PZIP	
ACADEMY	High school from which the student graduated. In our church school system, secondary schools are commonly called academies. They are always co-ed, never military.
PROFOBJECT	Career goal—anything from astronaut to zoologist.
ID	ID number used for administrative purposes. We do not use Social Security Number as a primary identifier.
PRIVACY	Flag="Y" if this student has requested not to be listed in directories. The lookup program will beep and put a special message on the screen if such a record is encountered. We average about one such record at a time among current students.
PPHONE	Parent telephone number
FALL_HRS	Number of hours this student took in the Fall semester included in this database.
WINT_HRS	Number of hours this student took in the Winter semester included in this database.

SUMM_HRS

Number of hours this student took during all sessions in the summer data included in this database.

For each class listed for each student, a record in the STUCLAS file contains:

PID

Used as a key identifying the student in this file. Obtained from the STUDENT file.

SECLASSNUM

Identifier of the class composed of a semester and a 4-digit identifier that appears in the class schedule.

For each class any student has taken, a record in the CLASS file contains:

SECLASSNUM

Identifier of the class composed of a semester and a 4-digit identifier that appears in the class schedule.

CLASSNAME

Such as "Intro to Public Speaking."

DEPARTMENT

Four-character code identifying the department offering the class.

COURSENUM

For "Intro to Public Speaking," this is the number 135.

SECTION

If we have more than one section of the class, this is the section identifier.

BEGINTIME

Hour and minute the class begins

ENDTIME

. . . and ends

DAYS

Six-character string with flags for each day on which the class is offered. We have no classes on Saturday.

ROOM

Identifier for where the class is offered, which generally has a 3-character code for the building and three characters for the room number.

TEACHER

The primary teacher of the class.

HOURS

How many credit hours the class offers.

SESSION

For summer school classes, which session this class is in. We have separate sessions in May, June, July, and August.

WRITECOD

Flag indicating whether this class meets the requirement for exercising the student's writing abilities.

CLCOMMENT

Other information such as "Meets first half of semester only."

Before you implement your own system just like ours, note that at different campuses different information may be considered private. At the secondary school attached to Southern College, for instance, the birth year is considered directory information—two levels from its position at Southern. On the other hand, Southern has only recently restricted class schedules. Until 1988, any person who wanted to find a student could walk up to the Registrar's office desk and flip through a master class schedule of all students in school. At many institutions class schedules are considered so sensitive that even campus safety personnel may not access them on a routine basis. Our list of data may be useful to you—but only as a point of departure in your discussions.

INDEXES

Each of these files is endowed with indexes permitting rapid access using any imaginable key. The use of indexes combines the advantages of relationality with high efficiency.

The double listing of major and minor is technically a violation of relational database theory. This violation creates a problem when indexes are generated: if a person has two majors, she/he would normally only be listed with her/his first major in the major index. As a work-around, we have a special program that "double-stuffs" the major and minor indexes so that all students with a given major (or minor) will appear in the index regardless of whether the listing of that major is primary or secondary. This is a highly technical detail, but has profound implications for how you use the data. It can also cause difficulty when the BROWSE functions of certain database software are used. The solution is simple: if the index we provide doesn't work properly, the user makes her/his own.

LOOKUP

To give easy access to this wealth of data, we created a special computer program that is distributed along with the data files. Equipment specifications include an IBM PC or compatible with at least 640K bytes of RAM, and 3 megabytes of available hard disk space. LOOKUP runs acceptably on an 8088-based computer, very fast on an 80286, and instantly on anything faster. Using LOOKUP, one can pull up a student and her/his class schedule in about a second knowing only the roommate's name (Figure 7.2). LOOKUP will also generate printed data for an individual student, or a list of students in a specific class. LOOKUP is written in Turbo Pascal using Skipjack for database access.

Downloading the data into these files is a multistep procedure. A batch run on our administrative computer extracts data into flat files, then downloads them into a PC that is used to prepare the master copy of this database. Finally, it invokes a batch run on the PC that reloads the DBF and NDX files with data from the flat files.

```
ID 18274 Public ID 2817            Advisor BAKER, JOHN E.              DEGREE BA
NAME Hendrickson, Kenneth           MAJOR EPSY                        MINOR
PREFNAME Kenny                      PNAME Mr & Mrs John Hendrickson
SADR1                               PADR1
SADR2 304 Talge Hall               PADR2 146 Lee Highway
SCITY Collegedale,                  PCITY Portland,                   (615) 325-7218
SSTATE TN      SZIP 37315           PSTATE TN      PZIP 37148
RES    M304 TELEPHONE ( ) 238-3304  ACADEMY HIGHLAND AC
SEX    M    BD 0130    HRS F:16 W:16  S: 6   PROFOBJECT TCHG ELEM              F92
```

SCLNM CLASSNAME	DEPT	CNUM	S	H s	TIME	DAYS			ROOM	TEACHER
3007 INTRO TO EDUCATION	EDUC	135	A	3	0800	M	W	F	SH106	BABCOCK, GEO
4965 ADVENTIST HERITAGE	RELT	138	A	3	0900	M	W	F	BH217	DU PREEZ, RO
2871 INTR PUBLIC SPEAKING	SPCH	135	B	3	1000	M	W	F	BH347	DICK, DONALD
5122 CONCERT BAND	MUPF	128		1	1100	M	W	F	JMW214	SILVER, PATR
3760 DEVELOPMENTAL PSYC	PSYC	128	B	3	0930		T	T	SH106	BANDIOLA, BE
5720 INTERMED SPANISH I	SPAN	211	B	3	1400		T	T	BH343	OTT, HELMUT
		Total:		16						

```
Action (F1=Help,   F2=Print,   F3/4=Fall,   F5/6=Wint,   F7/8=Summ, PgUp,PgDn,Esc):_
```

Student Lookup Screen. See data descriptions for meanings of fields.
Actions:

F1:	Help screen
F2:	Print data from top part of screen
F3:	Display fall class schedule on screen
F4:	Print fall class schedule on printer
F5:	Display winter class schedule on screen
F6:	Print winter class schedule on printer
F7:	Display summer class schedule on screen
F8:	Print summer class schedule on printer
PgUp	Display previous student in index order selected
PgDn	Display next student in index order selected

Figure 7.2   Student Lookup Screens (see data descriptions for meanings of fields)

PACKAGING

So far, we had a program that would work just fine—on a network. Now for the creative part: getting it to our users. For sending a piece of shareware to a colleague, it is enough to copy it onto a floppy disk and stick it in intermail. But we were dealing with secretaries who never "have the time" to do anything technically demanding. This much data would have to be compressed, and in some cases require multiple disks. Yet SCOOP must be easy enough for them to install themselves, and appear impressive enough to get them to install it. We put as much work into distribution packaging as we did into the development of the database and LOOKUP program combined.

The initial package delivered to a user comes in a high-quality PC-style binder with neatly printed documentation and plastic pages to hold the current update disks. This package goes a long way toward establishing the value of the product in the minds of our users.

Since the inquiry program itself is highly self-documenting, our users rarely refer to the documentation once SCOOP is on their computers. The binder serves primarily as a place to keep the floppy disks, and as a reminder of one of the uses they have for their computers. It sits on the user's shelf along with the many other books that bespeak their academic lifestyle.

The INSTALL program is designed to make it as easy as possible for users to do their own loading of the database. It asks for configuration information, providing defaults (i.e.; load from A: into C:\SCOOP) that work for virtually all our users. It then erases the current data on the user's computer and uses a decompression program to load the data from the installation diskette(s), prompting them to insert additional disks if and when needed.

The entire process takes less than five minutes. With a little prodding the first few times, we find all of our users installing their copies of the database themselves.

DISTRIBUTION

Bill Estep, our Operations Manager, is a very organized person. That is a useful trait when you are distributing software to people who have a wide variety of equipment. He has entered each SCOOP recipient in a database with information on each one's desired disk format and whether she/he gets SCOOP, MCD (see below), or both. This database is used to print professional-quality labels on distribution disks, and envelopes that get SCOOP to recipients properly. He also functions as our "alpha" tester—finding bugs before we distribute them to users. All this work has a great deal to do with the project's success.

RESULTS

SCOOP has been very well received. It has largely quieted requests for remote terminals on our administrative computer. Indeed, the lookup program is so powerful that several users who have direct connections to the administrative system use SCOOP instead for much of their work.

One day a recruitment team was visiting from a university to which we feed many of our graduates. While in a faculty member's office, the team members asked how they could get in touch with a certain senior. The faculty member pulled SCOOP up on his PC, and printed out the student's address and current class information. His visitors wondered how he got enough priority to have such fantastic service from our "mainframe." He was happy to show them that it all comes in on a floppy disk.

Other uses have surfaced. Our Energy Management department uses the data to plan distribution of energy to buildings so they do not consume energy needlessly, yet are comfortable for classes. We have added export interfaces to the LOOKUP program so that teachers who use computer-based grade books do not have to type in name lists. We have found SCOOP to be an excellent product to place on any newly-installed PC, so that a new user will have something useful to do immediately with her/his new computer.

SCOOP is especially popular in the Music Department, which frequently must locate the members of musical groups to schedule rehearsals and performances. The Music Department likes the LOOKUP program's interface so much that we have patterned its record library inquiry facility after it. The department keeps its primary copy of the data on its library's PC using Alpha 4, Version 2 for updating. A batch creates distribution disks to get the data moved to the department's other computers. This guarantees that hackers playing with the student inquiry station cannot damage the department's original data. Just like SCOOP, the department has the functionality it desires from a network without the cost.

The dormitories have an application for SCOOP that is less popular in some circles. When dormitory students fill out weekend leave requests detailing where they are going and who they are going with, one copy of the form is on postcard stock. SCOOP is used to make a label that sends this copy to the students' parents.

FUTURE DEVELOPMENT

With a large number of disks to produce at times that are already busy for us, we are looking for ways to improve the efficiency of distribution. We are encouraging departments to share a single set of disks (perhaps detailing a student worker to install it on all applicable computers). Another project is to reduce the number of double-density disks being distributed, since they multiply the effort needed as compared to high density. We regularly survey these users to see if their equipment has been upgraded so we can give them higher density (and fewer) disks. Our plans for a campus network will definitely include electronic SCOOP distribution.

Many departments wish grades were also available. We feel that this may come with time, although controls will be necessary. For the moment, grades are distributed to departments through microfiche. Our Records Office has some valid concerns about floppy disk distribution of grade information. Grades have a broader potential for invading privacy than class schedules. They are permanent in nature, so a given set of data has potential for damage over a longer period of time. It is also easier to copy large amounts of information from floppy disks than from a microfiche. One possibility would be distributing grades only to people who have a valid interest in them. An advisor might only get grades for his/her advisees, for instance. Or a department might only get grades for majors they have. But the primary use of grades in a department is in evaluating prospective majors. So the debate over who should have access to which grades continues.

We have had several requests that we include a report generator in the LOOKUP program. Currently the only reports it will print provide data for a single student, and a list of the members of a single class. The requests we have generally take the form such as "Print an alphabetical list of all students with majors x, y, and z who are sophomores or above." While we are taking this request seriously, we also recognize that it is an indication that the program is headed in the right direction.

TIMING

A complaint we heard when first proposing floppy disk distribution of the SCOOP program is that it is not truly online access. We have countered this concern by selecting distribution dates at strategic points in the academic year. For the first month of Fall and Winter Semesters, we issue a SCOOP update each week. The rest of the year it is monthly. Updates during the summer are scheduled to correspond with significant points in our summer session cycle. This update cycle has satisfied most of our customers. We have several, however, who need an initial update in the very first few days of the semester. So we have established a "hot list" of those who should get the special preview issue of SCOOP.

DISTRIBUTION

Since a significant segment of our SCOOP users are actually connected to the administrative computer, we are considering loading the compressed files back onto the administrative computer for downloading, instead of requiring us to make as many floppy disks. An alternative might be a central BBS from which people could get the current update at any time. Either of these would decrease the friendliness of our current installation system, but would give the people more timely data.

CAN YOU DO THIS FOR STUDENTS?

Almost as an afterthought, we developed a directory-only subset of SCOOP. It is distributed on the same cycle. We call it MCD (**M**icrocomputer **D**irectory). It is available for students on the library's card catalog network, and is a very popular option there. Campus clubs wishing to mail materials to students often prefer the information in computerized form.

CONCLUSION

If you want to set up a network, don't wait to bring up applications. You may find that you can do exciting things without any network at all. By thinking about what we would do if we had a campus-wide network, we have found new ways to be useful to our clients. SCOOP will probably change as our campus needs change. It will be the first deliverable product on our campus-wide network. But SCOOP will always be remembered as the network we had before we had a network.

We will be happy to provide a demonstration copy of the student version of our student directory database for a $10.00 reproduction fee. We'll include source code for the LOOKUP and data conversion programs. Request item "MCD Demo," and send a check or purchase order to:

> Attn: John Beckett
> Information Services Department
> Southern College of SDA
> P. O. Box 370
> Collegedale, TN 37315

SOFTWARE USED

Alpha 4: Alpha Software Corporation, One North Avenue, Burlington, MA 01803 (617) 229-2924. This is an excellent database for nonprogrammers. Works very well with SCOOP. I use it for debugging and design work. Our Music Department uses it for managing its record library database, which has over 35,000 entries.

Powerhouse: Every administrative computer should have some kind of high-level language that can be used to extract and reformat data rapidly. We used Cognos' QUIZ, a component of its Powerhouse 4GL on the HP 3000. If you don't have a 4GL, get one.

Skipjack: Max Software Consultants, Inc., 4101 Greenmount Avenue, Baltimore, MD 21218 (301) 828-5935. This is a library of procedures that delivers dBase programming functions to Turbo Pascal. If I read Borland's literature correctly, this functionality is included in some of its new software.

Turbo Pascal: Borland International, 1800 Green Hills Road/P. O. Box 660001, Scotts Valley, CA 95067-0001 (408) 438-5300. My native tongue, when programming on microcomputers. I suppose I'll have to learn C one of these days, because that is where things are headed.

Turbo Professional: Turbo Power Software, P. O. Box 66747, Scotts Valley, CA 95066-0747 (408) 438-8600. Used to put together quickly a user interface menu system. If it included dBase access, it would be perfect.

Chapter Eight

DESIGNING AND MANAGING A DIVISION-WIDE NETWORK: TECHNICAL AND ORGANIZATIONAL ISSUES

Gary D. Malaney
Assistant Professor, Higher Education; Director, Student Affairs Research, Information, & Systems, University of Massachusetts

Rosio Alvarez
Research Assistant
School of Management, University of Massachusetts

Sampson (1982, p. 40) observed that "almost every area of student personnel is relying on computers in some way to enhance available services." He also noted several standard problems with which administrators must deal, such as lack of adequate software, staff anxiety and negative attitudes toward computing, access and privacy issues, incompatible hardware and software, and waste of resources.

Today, there is probably an even greater reliance on computer technology within student affairs (Baier & Strong, in press). In addition to all of the concerns mentioned by Sampson, however, many higher education and student affairs administrators face major budgetary cutbacks. Lack of resources produces a problem in maintaining adequate technical personnel to train users and in providing technical support for the adequate utilization of the new technology.

Several studies report a relatively high level of problems with microcomputer usage mainly due to the lack of user support services and of training, and poor responsiveness of computing specialists (Benson, 1983; Rockart and Flannery, 1984; Danziger and Kraemer, 1986). Therefore, successful implementation of computer technology includes providing assistance in organizational learning and change needed to make new office tools most beneficial (Pava, 1983).

Much of the literature available on administrative local area networks focuses on the technical issues of implementation, such as network operating systems, topology, platforms, interconnectivity, and applications development

(Halaris and Sloan, 1989; Bates and Leclerc, 1989; Weaver, 1991). And although these issues are critical in a successful implementation, they are not sufficient. The discussion should be expanded to encompass organizational issues, such as sustained technical support, training of users, and fostering communications and cooperation between users and technical staff. Therefore, the purpose of this chapter is to present an overview of a successful implementation of interconnected local area networks on a division-wide level. The Division of Student Affairs at the University of Massachusetts at Amherst is the subject of this discussion, which goes beyond technological issues and includes organizational issues within the context of austere budgetary times.

BACKGROUND AND COMPUTING ENVIRONMENT

The University of Massachusetts at Amherst (UMA) has full-time enrollment of 23,000 (17,000 undergraduate and 6,000 graduate students). The Division of Student Affairs is responsible for providing services to the student population. These services include housing, financial aid, admissions, career placement, academic support, and student activities, to name a few. The coordination of information between these departments is crucial in providing efficient services to such a large population of students. Consequently, increasing the utilization of computers as tools for data sharing within the division is the logical and inevitable path to follow.

In 1984, the Division of Student Affairs at UMA centralized its computer support for both mainframe and personal computing. The departments throughout the division relied heavily on administrative data residing on a IBM 3084, and support was scattered throughout the division. The staff of the Office of Student Affairs Research, Information, and Systems (SARIS) has been coordinating this centralized effort as it attempts to stay abreast of the ever-changing computer technology.

Several years ago, Student Affairs led the movement away from mainframe computing with the purchase of a Wang minicomputer primarily to serve the word processing needs of its staff in the Administration Building. While that system functioned fine for years, in 1988 the staff opted for the more powerful and flexible personal computer (PC) environment. The process of replacing the minicomputer workstations with PCs was gradual but consistent. Slowly the division acquired standalone PCs in various offices. During and after the migration from the minicomputer to standalone PCs, connectivity to the mainframe was via IRMA coax adapter boards and 3270 emulation software. Each PC required a board and coaxial connection to the mainframe controller. The mainframe controller ports are charged to each department by the data processing department.

In 1989, the computing environment within the division consisted of standalone PCs for word processing and spreadsheet applications and minimal use of the Wang minicomputer for limited word processing. During that year the

Admissions Office developed the first work-group LAN within Student Affairs. The development was prompted by an impending move of the Admissions Office from the Administration Building, where Admissions had direct coaxial connections to the administrative mainframe for data entry and look-up purposes. There were also direct connections to the Wang minicomputer for some word processing needs.

Prior to the Admissions work-group LAN, a 3-node LAN had been installed in Admissions in order to run the new transfer credit evaluation software that had been developed by SARIS (Walter and Malaney, 1991). A complete business analysis by SARIS staff and a re-seller, System Software Support, Inc., was conducted. The decision was made to implement a 20-node Novell network. This was to be the first of nine LAN's to be installed in Student Affairs.

TECHNICAL ISSUES

Over the past three years Student Affairs computing has grown to include a complex system of nine interconnected LANs (Figure 8.1). It is beyond the scope of this chapter to detail all technical aspects of each LAN work group. Therefore only selected cases are discussed, and technical specifics are described as they relate to these cases during the earlier growth period, or decentralization stage.

The Decentralization Stage

Admissions. The design chosen for Admissions was a thin coaxial ethernet bus topology network with twenty nodes. Netware SFT 2.15 was selected and installed on a 80286 file server. Since Admissions relied heavily on access to mainframe data, the LAN-to-mainframe link was accomplished by installing an SDLC remote gateway with a 9.6K-bps modem and PCOX software for terminal emulation.

SARIS. During the Admissions LAN design and installation, SARIS staff members were integral, and the experience gained in that effort was utilized in the design of SARIS's LAN within the Administration Building. The major impetus for the SARIS network, however, was the decision to replace the Wang minicomputer which had an annual maintenance cost exceeding $18,000 and was considered inefficient.

The design for SARIS's LAN was similar to that of Admissions, with the exception that the file server was a 80386 and the gateway an SNA coax mux 40-session device. This gateway uses multiplexing and was able to support forty sessions on a single card. The gateway allows forty sessions while only requiring five controller ports on the front-end processor. As IRMA adapter boards were pulled out, network interface cards were slotted into the existing PCs.

Financial Aid Services. The installation of the Financial Aid Services LAN was in response to a crisis. In the early spring of 1990 the department found itself unable to use its traditional third party mainframe software to process prospective applicants for the Fall of 1990. The software required an annual update that had been delayed by the vendor; consequently, implementation and testing had not begun. The deadline for processing was crucial as prospective students must have financial aid information when deciding among schools. The solution to the problem was to install a four-node Novell network that would run a microcomputer-based financial aid software package called MicroFAIDS. This would allow counselors to work on processing incoming students on the LAN. The information would then be uploaded to the mainframe when that system had been updated.

During this time the University was installing an Ericsson PBX; therefore, the wiring for the network was performed by the Telecommunications Office, which was responsible for wiring the data/voice system. The cabling was unshielded twisted pair (Lattisnet). Since the Financial Aid Services office was moving into the old location of the Admissions office, which required all new telephone installations, the opportunity to wire all telephone jacks for network connections was seized. The telecommunications office was instrumental in performing the needed cross-wiring. Telecommunications cross-wired all B telephone jacks at the IDF punch down block, to an external IDF punch down block accessible to the users. At that point the re-seller, Systems Software Support, cross-wired all connections, leaving patch cords available for the users to connect as they added workstations. The connections were made to several Synoptics 2510 Lattisnet concentrators that, in turn, were connected to the Financial Aid fileserver.

The approach of cross-wiring all telephone jacks gives users much flexibility without calling on "technical support." However, the increased flexibility was at the cost of constant coordination since this was a learning process for SARIS staff, the re-seller, and the telecommunications office.

Other Departments. Soon after the networks for Admissions, SARIS, and Financial Aid Services were installed, smaller departments within the administration building were interested in networking their resources. Because most of these offices were small, however, the implementation of a LAN was prohibitively expensive. The solution was to incorporate those offices through an approach similar to that of Financial Aid Services. For offices interested in networking their resources, the B telephone jacks were cross-wired by Telecommunications and then the re-seller. Concentrators were then installed and connected to existing LANs. To add a workstation required only a simple connection of the patch cord corresponding to the B jack for the workstation to an available concentrator port.

The cost of incorporating the workstation was the cost of the network interface card (NIC) if a port on the concentrator was available. Each concentrator allows for several workstation connects. One can also cascade (connect in series) for maximizing port availability. The ability to use UTP versus coaxial connectors was so attractive that SARIS changed many of its coaxial connections to UTP. The coaxial NICs were used with Lattisnet transceivers to convert from coax to UTP.

With the implementation of these LANs, it became obvious that tremendous computing power was available in a microcomputer network environment, and soon other Student Affairs offices located outside of the administration building wanted to employ the technology to establish their own work-group local area networks. SARIS staff members, in conjunction with Systems Software Support, Inc., designed systems for those interested offices.

The Centralization Stage

As the proliferation of LANs continued in Student Affairs, the issue of redundancy surfaced. For example, offices with work-group LANs that wanted access to the mainframe had to install their own gateways even if only a few individuals required the service. The sharing of resources and technical support was also very difficult in a physically disbursed environment. Toward that end, SARIS began to interconnect all planned and existing LANs. The technology employed to interconnect the existing networks consisted of remote and local bridges. The reintegration stage took place prior to the installation of fiber optic cabling between buildings so the alternative was to use leased lines from the PBX for the remote bridges. At the suggestion of the reseller, Link/64 remote bridges with synchronous V.35 boards were installed. Dedicated 386sx machines were used at each end with high speed terminal access units (TAUs) attached. Since data across the bridge would be screens for mainframe look ups, downloads, and e-mail, the 64K bps data transmission rate was adequate. Retix bridges were used for local bridges, to connect LANs within the same building.

SARIS also installed a communication server with a pool of four TAUs. This was in response to requests for external access to services such as the Internet or private networks and to the request from several remote offices for access to the LAN. The communication server has two Cubix boards for asynchronous remote access. Each board has two 80286s available for remote access. This allows the small offices in remote sites to dial in and use the 80286s to access the LAN. Additionally, the server allows two lines for dial out capability. Installing a communication server reduced the cost of installing TAUs at every PC on the network that desired dial-out access. Soon after SARIS installation of the Cubix communication server, Admissions followed with a similar system.

PRACTICAL APPLICATIONS

The many offices depicted in Figure 8.1 have widely ranging uses for the LAN and division-wide networking technology, but most of the offices with LANs use them for several standard applications, including word processing, spreadsheets, and mainframe access via the bridges and gateways for look-ups and file transfers. Several offices also utilize desktop publishing applications, graphics software, and small database applications for record keeping. A few offices have unique functions depending upon the type of service they perform.

For instance, as mentioned earlier, the Admissions Office has a LAN-based software application which was programmed by SARIS staff to assist in transfer credit evaluation. With this application, courses from the transcripts of transfer student applicants are entered into the computer, course equivalency tables are accessed, and course equivalences are assigned to a student's record electronically (Walter and Malaney, 1991). This process allows the Admissions Office to provide transfer applicants with a list of the UMA course equivalences for the accepted transfer courses at the time of notification of admission. The Admissions Office also enters all of the data from student applications via the LAN and then transmits the data to the mainframe student database in large batches. This process increases the control that the Admissions Office has over the data before it goes to the mainframe database.

Housing Services has developed an online system in which disciplinary records are entered into computers located in the cluster offices of the residence hall system and then sent electronically to the central Housing Office. When necessary, the files also can be transferred electronically to the Dean of Students' Office for further action.

The Career Center has the opportunity to use another LAN-based application developed by SARIS staff to assist in matching student job candidates with prospective employers. With this application, data regarding job openings from specific employers are obtained and entered by the Career Center staff in conjunction with data from graduating students seeking employment. Items including type of job, required skills, and location are run through a computer matching program. The resulting matches can then be displayed for the Career Center staff to be used in counseling students.

The Financial Aid Services office has student programmers that have developed prototypes on the network for large scale mainframe applications using C or Pascal. These prototypes are then used by Data Processing programmers for developing large scale Cobol programs. Additionally, programs that allow electronic data transmittals to loan agencies for expediting student loan processing have been developed.

SARIS has utilized the LAN to develop and test LAN-based software applications for other offices within Student Affairs. In addition to coordinating computing activity for Student Affairs, SARIS also coordinates the research operation for Student Affairs, so the office has some unique computer needs pertaining to its research function. One of the most common uses of the SARIS LAN is by Project Pulse, the telephone survey research operation, which uses a software package that allows data entry during the survey process via electronic questionnaires (Thurman and Malaney, 1989). Once these raw data are collected, they are built into a data file using SPSS-PC. Analyses are run, graphs and charts are prepared, and text is written. The whole report is prepared through desktop publishing software and is then printed for dissemination.

One of the primary reasons for the development of the division-wide area network is to allow paper-free communication within the entire division of Student Affairs. Some of the offices with LANs are already utilizing electronic mail packages to communicate. As soon as the division-wide network is completed, the entire division will be able to use electronic mail. Simple messages, memos, letters, and entire documents will be easily transferred across the division-wide area network.

ORGANIZATIONAL ISSUES

As Figure 8.1 shows SARIS became the "hub" for the division-wide network. This was partially due to the role played by SARIS staff from the early stages but also due to organizational reasons. As mentioned earlier SARIS was charged with the responsibility to assist in all forms of computer activity throughout the Division and serve a coordinating role in the collection and distribution of information pertaining to computer systems. Any office or department needing computer assistance is supposed to utilize the resources within SARIS. It is important to note that SARIS's role is not to infringe on the autonomy of departmental computer activity. The purpose is to provide a central resource for collecting and distributing information regarding such issues as hardware and software technology, applications development, personnel, funding and resource allocation, and division-wide computing standards. SARIS recognizes the need and advantages of distributive computing for the individual Student Affairs departments but also provides a common linkage for sharing among those departments.

Another reason for having a central clearinghouse is to ensure compatibility within the Division whether it be for hardware or software. Software compatibility is crucial because there must be limits regarding the number of different types of PCs and software packages if there is to be appropriate support centrally. For instance, when everyone in the Division is using the same word processing or spreadsheet packages, staff support for training and troubleshooting is much simpler.

SARIS became the central hub for information and technical assistance partly due to the implementation strategy as well. Most of the expansion of the division-wide network occurred during the initial phases of UMA's austere budgetary times, so SARIS opted to use its technical staff to perform as much of the implementation, configuration, and maintenance as possible. At the time, this allowed maximum expansion with minimum funds. As technical staff left and vacancies were not filled, however, the lack of technical support and training became critical.

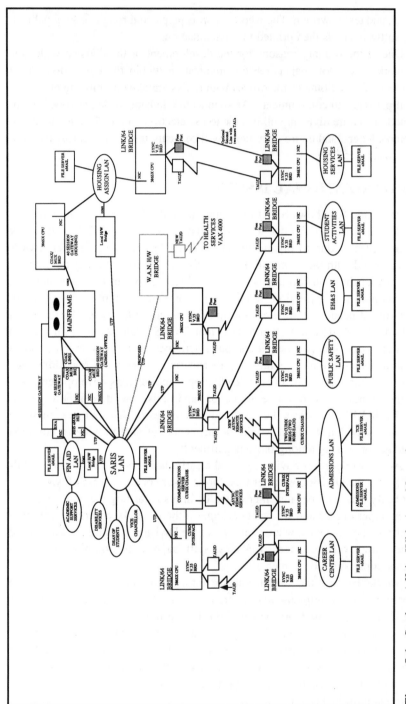

Figure 8.1   Student Affairs Wide Area Network

In response to the understaffing of technical personnel, the Manager of Financial Aid Systems and the Director of SARIS formed a *Student Apprenticeship Program*. This program was designed to recruit and intensively train a few undergraduate students to act as LAN administrators. The students were carefully selected, with criteria such as good academic standing, year in school (only sophomores or juniors), technical major, prior experience and good references, employed. These students were paid above the normal wages earned by students on campus, or off. Students were then intensively trained by the Manager of Financial Aid Systems who had participated extensively in the expansion of the division-wide network. The students were trained for approximately one semester then placed in offices that were in need of technical support. The Director of SARIS coordinated the recruitment and subsequent placement. The apprenticeship program encouraged peers to work together even after placement. The program was so successful that one of the more advanced students became an instructor for the students entering in the following year.

In general, the students were the only alternative for providing technical support and in some respects, the best. They maintained an interest in new technology, acquired difficult technical concepts with relative ease, and kept well-read with regard to current trends in computing. The experience they gained was important for their future career placement. Additionally, the permanent staff's response to student technical support was well received. The students worked well as trainers and did not intimidate users, perhaps because they were students and not professional staff members. Consequently, even during the most difficult budgetary times, Student Affairs computing was well managed and supported.

THE IMPORTANCE OF CONTINUED MANAGEMENT AND PLANNING

As this chapter shows, managing the division-wide area network within Student Affairs is not a simple task, nor is it without cost. Depending on the size of the operation and the extent of the computer system, its management is easily a full-time job for at least one individual, if not an entire staff. Coordination of the activities among departments and an overall systems plan are important factors in cost-effective resource management which, in turn, should assist in improving services to students. Without computerization, such activities as admissions, financial aid, and registration would take considerably longer than they do now. Before the existence of extensive computerization, staff members spent more time interacting with paper than with students. Through the implementation and continued management of division-wide area networks, Student Affairs staff was better able to provide services to students.

ACKNOWLEDGEMENT

Acknowledgements are due Judy Connelly, Joe Fitzgerald, and SSS, Inc. for their continued assistance in developing and maintaining the division-wide network and Judy Connelly and SSS, Inc. for their work in preparing Figure 8.1.

REFERENCES

Bates, J. & Leclerc, G. (1989). Reaching the promised LAN. *Proceedings of the CAUSE National Conference*. San Diego, CA.

Benson, D. H. (1983). A field study of end user computing: Findings and issues. *MIS Quarterly* 6(4), 35-45.

Danziger, J. N. & Kraemer, K. L. (1986). *People and computers: The impacts of computing on end users in organizations*. New York: Columbia University Press.

Halaris, A. S. & Sloan, L. W. (1989). An implemented strategy for campus connectivity and cooperative computing. *Cause/Effect*, 12(4), 36-41.

Pava, C. H. P. (1983). *Managing new office technology: An organizational strategy*. New York: Free Press.

Rockart, J. F. & Flannery, L. S. (1983). The management of end user computing. *Communications of the ACM*, 26(10), 776-784.

Sampson, J. P. Jr. (1982). Effective computer resource management: Keeping the tail from wagging the dog. *NASPA Journal*, 19(3), 38-46.

Baier, J. L. & Strong, T. S. (Eds.). (in press). *Technology in student affairs: Using high-tech to enhance high-touch*. Alexandria, VA: ACPA Media Board.

Thurman, Q. and Malaney, G.D. (1989). Surveying students as a means of assessing and changing policies and practices of student affairs programs, *NASPA Journal*, 27(2), 101-107.

Walter, M. P. & Malaney, G. D. (1991). A transfer credit evaluation system for a stand alone personal computer or a local area network, *College and University*, 66(2), 95-104.

Weaver, M. (1991). Providing distributed strategies with centralized resources: A case study. *Proceedings of the CAUSE National Conference*. Anaheim, CA.

PART TWO

Client/Server Models: Distributing the Power

CHAPTER NINE

MOVING TOWARDS A CLIENT/SERVER MODEL FOR ADMINISTRATIVE COMPUTING

Dr. Lloyd A. Case
Director of Information Technology
California State University Stanislaus

We like thinking that every university follows the same trail in moving from central mainframe support to distributed client/server architecture computing. Our experiences would not fit the standard model. Still, variation in the trails we take can give additional understanding of the trip.

California State University Stanislaus has a central computing office using a mainframe, but we are far from centralized in our model of administrative information systems. Important computing support such as payroll, faculty work load reporting, and the development of financial accounting systems, comes from other systems miles away in other state agencies. Nonetheless, we do not view our administrative systems as distributed.

Over the last two years our campus administrators in finance, student records, personnel, public safety, student services, and physical plant functions met and studied all current systems. Strong motivations appeared to improve and update them. The study yielded a surprising self-picture. We identified the issues we must tackle to achieve our client/server model.

The relative percentage of central mainframe use compared with all computing use has decreased. Mainframe workloads grew in absolute terms, but lean budget years caused delays in central facility response to user requests. Central computing office's inability to support growth aggressively did not stop offices from wanting better systems or needing productivity increases. So, those offices addressed their own computing needs. Microcomputers, LANs, and consultants appeared all over campus.

83

The pragmatic office-based efforts used low-cost technology. People saw them as temporary fixes. These solutions lacked integration and wide accessibility. Coordination consisted of a purchase justification process and a campus standard for hardware.

We use the Apple Macintosh (Mac) as a standard. This one standard has served remarkably well. At first, it provided sharing of laser printers and files. It prepared us to unite our LANs with a campus Ethernet. The mainframe and campus network now work together to serve offices through AppleTalk LANs and Ethernet. We have benefited as various opportunities from Apple and third parties for FTP transfers, TN3270 emulations, security, and database products such as Oracle came into the market. Also, we have shared expertise between offices in our planning processes because of this common denominator.

The Macs emulate terminals to communicate with the mainframe. Extracts of data on the mainframe go to the LAN and then the Mac. These are Microsoft Excel and Word documents. Standard ASCII files are simple to share too. Once data enters the Mac, statistical analyses, summaries, etc., for projects execute there. Much real computing work happens this way—the mainframe serves as a fileserver with interactive online data entry stored. Meanwhile, it continues its classical support for campus student records and financial accounting.

Concrete reasons for change became evident: the accounting office must migrate computer systems to a required new financial accounting code. The code runs neither on the current mainframe nor on LANs. We want to replace our old mainframe because of its large maintenance and operating costs. We lack integration in our patchwork of pragmatic systems, causing problems every day. We estimate over half our backlog comes from this patchwork and by the daily office changes. Changes create a moving target for proposed enhancements.

Some reasons for change came from experience with the office-based systems. For example, a once exciting cashiering system written by a faculty member and his students needed fixing. No one sold the disk drives anymore and even used drives became extinct. The application code was in assembler code. No one could find the source code nor the student. It was no longer possible to extend or patch this system. Similar things happened in the purchasing system and in the position control system. Four to five years was the life span of several of our office-based solutions.

Client/server computing using open systems is attractive from a technological price and performance view. The best attraction was its natural recasting of our environment. We expected to use its modular nature for episodes of development made necessary by our unpredictable finances. We will not make the total commitment to a single vendor and schedule necessary in the strategy of "integrating by purchase-commitment." We expect episodes of development for financial systems, student systems, and personnel systems. Integration will come by following our campus plan. Episodes of client/server modules will better fit our constraints in a state system of multiple support offices, dictated code requirement, flighty funding, and political pressures.

Our twelve months of examination showed a big gap between our pragmatically dispersed information model and a coordinated client/server model.

USERS CONSIDER DISTRIBUTION OF COMPUTING SYSTEMS

"Distribute computing!" was the theme in many of the early meetings. User cries for client-server technology seemed identical to distributed computing. The task force struggled to define user needs and what "distribute" or "client/server" meant to them.

At first offices said they wanted better price:performance. That was all. To many, a client-server model defined a cost-efficient technology. We had now to separate trade journal and marketing information from a clear understanding of our need and our project costs.

Quickly it was clear cost savings were not the sole need. The users were not technology chasers interested only in price:performance. They wanted their office work to go better. This meant effective information support must provide more responsiveness, more functionality, friendlier use. To them, this meant support that they controlled, prioritized, and operated.

They described initiating jobs, fast query of data, extraction of data blocks, quick processing of information, flexible responses to their needs and those of their bosses. Users were more confident of doing this in their own offices using their own microcomputers under their own time schedules. Such it was that "distribution" meant to them.

This was not the end of the evolution of our thinking.

Responsiveness and user control don't logically require machine and/or data to relocate to several sites or to numerous servers. A look at higher education today shows that mainframe-based systems of adequate size can provide them. Are we only looking for more modern systems?

Once office-based pragmatic answers were in operation, they hit the same wall that stymied central computing services: limited resources, unlimited information needs. Users believe the computer center has money that they might share. Here was the Stage 2 of office-based systems. Negotiate accepting some central production work being done in offices, but obtain the central computing resources to do it and the next stage of growth in office-based systems. Money spent on new technology would cover the production need and give a windfall of resources on the margin.

We examined this scenario. At Stanislaus, the Office of Information Technology (computer center) has twenty people and an annual budget of $1.4 million. This would supply many PCs and give new positions to many offices.

Much of this budget is in staff costs. Just how does the Information Technology office use this staff? We found that two keep the campus instructional television running for 32 classes; two keep the campus cable plant for TV, telephones, and digital services. One person runs a UNIX server, designs networks, and troubleshoots network services and e-mail for over a thousand users. Two run student computer laboratories and two operate instructional media. Three people are analysts-programmers; one is a system support worker to the mainframe, three operators; two are managers; and two provide clerical support.

After some study of the job descriptions, the committee realized that most of these functions must continue in even a totally discontinued central computer support scenario. Functions such as telephone infrastructure work or accounting, night operations of computing systems, campus network cabling, e-mail and other campus network services, instructional computer laboratories shared by all disciplines, data clerk scheduling, television course production, and others, are difficult to imagine as spread across several offices. Information Technology was already "distributed" as far as logic allows.

We now recognize "distribution" of information systems to be a matrix spanned by the type of dispersion of the system and by the element of the system being dispersed, as shown in Table 9.1.

Table 9.1 Stanislaus' Types of Dispersion of IS Support			
SYSTEM ELEMENT	Not Dispersed	Dispersed in physical location	Dispersed in logical location
Processing	A	B	C
Data/Program code	D	E	F
Organization	G	H	I
Management	J	K	L
User Access	M	N	O

In this syntax, we view ourselves as an ADILNO-dispersed school moving to an CFIJO model. We believe the textbook dispersion model starts with ADGJO. Note that client server technology provides the possibility of dispersion. Client/server technology and system distribution are not equivalent terms by any means in our planning. The trick is to define objectives.

CALIFORNIA STATE UNIVERSITY STANISLAUS

Our medium sized university has about 4700 FTE (Full Time Equivalent) students, primarily in 4-year undergraduate programs, with another 1000 FTE in graduate programs. We are one of the twenty campuses of the California State University System. The CSU System enrolls over 350,000 FTE students each year.

System membership places requirements on information systems. Each campus must use a common—at the code level—financial information system. Each campus is individually responsible for its student records, course master files, and faculty work load reporting systems. All campuses have their origin in a common grandfather system created by the Chancellor's Office of Information Resources and Technology. Many personnel and all payroll computing for these twenty campuses happen at state government computer facilities in Sacramento, one hundred miles away. This dispersion of information systems makes an integrated information system for operation and management problematic.

Alumni and Giving systems operate on a Macintosh LAN resource in the campus Alumni Office.

In recent years the former monolithic computing support of the Chancellor's Office of Information Resources was distributed to campuses. All implementation, operation, and maintenance of information systems, except finance, went to campuses.

For a relatively small institution, this composite of distributed and centralist philosophies is unusual. Our size makes coordination difficult. Operations are not fully consistent, void of redundancy, nor synchronized well. Development not coordinated between agencies may clash in time of resource priorities. We do operate despite this, but our overhead in time and human effort is large—unusually so—for our size.

WHAT ARE OUR NEEDS?

In January of 1992, our Administrative Information Systems Planning group conducted a campus questionnaire. Responses came from over 85 percent of the campus administrative offices. Some academic departmental offices and all the academic deans also responded. The goal was to scope the nature, utility, and perceived adequacy of our many systems. We were at once surprised and mollified.

Overall Observations About Validity

The survey instrument was not perfect, nor scientifically administered. We attempted to remove concerns of statistical validity by inviting every office to participate and give opinions. This was not entirely successful since some offices did not respond or were missed in the process.

The major problem in this survey appears to be the questions themselves. They were technical enough that a few offices called to have the questions clarified. One can only guess at how many confused people did not call. Still, a majority seemed to follow instructions and respond in a way that indicates they believed they knew what was asked.

It does merit some thought before trusting this survey with answering a precise quantitative question. It would be reasonable to suspect that the survey does give some general or overall characteristics, rankings, and opinions.

Some Global Observations on the Responses

Although this survey concerned computerized information systems, the survey explicitly expanded its definitions to include noncomputer-based information systems. Also the survey includes office-based or PC-based systems. This survey should represent a compilation of all IS needed to operate Stanislaus.

The survey had five questions, covering 78 campus information systems. These systems should include all the current campus systems; however, we asked respondents to identify information systems they feel the list missed. They did so. They identified sixty-nine additional information systems. This suggests the survey only anticipated 53 percent of the existing systems!

This is misleading, however, since some of the entries volunteered were components of current systems, or enhancements to current systems rather than purely new information systems. Fully 22 of these 69 are new. Further, 41 of the 69 are enhancements. Compare this to the 78 standard IS systems given in the survey. Of these, 73 of 78 were critical to at least one office. Seven of the 78 were "critical" to ten or more offices.

Of the 69 volunteered IS additions, 34 were "critical" to the operation of at least one department office. The missing systems are important and must not be dismissed. What follows is restricted to observations for the standard 78 systems. This is because the "volunteered" 69 would not have a true comparison since not everyone was asked their opinions of these.

Question 1. Fill in a chart of named systems versus columns indicating if the respondent operates the system.

The number of offices operating an IS represents a total of all those responding offices that indicated they operated this system. There may have been some misunderstanding of this question but it seeks to identify who is responsible and budgeted to run each particular information system.

If the responses are correct, Stanislaus has several redundant systems, or responsibility is misunderstood. Three systems report four or more offices running them. Ten systems have three or more operating offices. Over one-third (28) have two or more offices operating them. Perhaps these offices each have a comparable system dealing with separate information, or perhaps they each feel responsible for some aspect of a single system, or they are confused as to who is responsible. There is a potential that the survey has found a problem of defined responsibility or of redundancy of systems and expenses.

Question 2. Fill in a chart of named systems versus columns indicating if the respondent uses the system.

This question seeks to see who benefits from the use of each system. We tallied those offices who responded they use information from the system.

Three systems have over 15 offices using them. Sixteen systems have ten offices using them.

This speaks strongly to the Stanislaus IS being complex and interrelated. (It was interesting that one dean's office responded it used none of the systems in any way. Presumably the office staff felt self sufficient and saw no need to work with a campus system. This office has three Macintosh microcomputers for word processing and e-mail.)

Question 3. Fill in a chart of named systems versus columns indicating if the respondent passes data to the system.

This seeks to identify who enters information into the collection of IS systems. Eleven of the 78 have only one office feeding data into them. This means 67 have at least two offices feeding data into them, and many have over a half-dozen offices supplying data.

The suggestion is quite strong here that our information systems are highly integrated and interrelated activities, with much interoffice cooperation and activity. This speaks strongly to the need for careful management and good networking.

Question 4. Fill in a chart of named systems versus columns indicating if the respondent values use of the system.

This question seeks a value judgment from the respondents. They rate individual systems on their usefulness to the office: "critical", "useful", "nice to have", or "no need."

Question 5. Fill in a chart of named systems versus columns indicating if the respondent feels the system is adequate and if it needs changing.

This question requires the office to agree or not with the statement that the specific system is adequate today. An answer of "agree" means the respondent sees no need for improvement or replacement.

Of those believing the individual systems were adequate, fewer were satisfied than dissatisfied. Table 9.2 shows the top "adequate systems." These ranged from 20 to 38 percent in descending order.

Table 9.2   Systems Rated Adequate at the Current Time by the January 1992 Information System Survey

System Name	Percent	System Name	Percent	System Name	Percent
Class Schedule	36	Phone Billing/ Reporting System	24	Audit Trail Requirements	21
Stores	26				
Accounts Payable	25	Cash Receipts/ Cashiering	23	Budgeting/Planning	21
Foundation	25	General Ledger	22	Keys Systems	20
Library Acq, Circ, Catalog, ILL Serv	24	Printing/Duplicating	22	Class Lists/	
		Accounts Receivable	21	Enrollments Reporting	19

Similarly the systems the respondents ranked as currently inadequate appear in descending order (Table 9.3). These range from 57 percent to 30 percent. The survey does not allow for collection of the rationale for the dissatisfaction. The reasons may vary considerably.

Table 9.3   Systems Rated Inadequate at the Current Time by the January 1992 Information System Survey

System Name	Percent
Student Records	57
Registration Processing	44
Class Lists/Enrollments Reporting	42
Procurement	36
Instit Research Systems Support	36
Accounts Receivable	36
Enrollment Projections	34
Facilities Scheduling	33
Inventory(financial mgmt)	33
Inventory(General, other)	33
Management Reporting	32
Accounts Payable	32
Personnel	32
Position Control	32
Reporting	31

Table 9.4   Currently Inadequate Critical Systems

System	A	B	C	D	E	F
Student Records	15	7	2	9	30	57
Registration Processing	9	5	1	14	25	44
Class Lists/Enroll Rpt	14	9	0	9	26	42
Procurement	5	5	0	18	25	36
Instit Research Systems	6	3	2	14	25	36
Accounts Receivable	11	5	2	11	28	36
Enrollment Projections	4	12	1	15	29	34
Facilities Scheduling	4	9	9	9	27	33
Inventory (finan. mgmt)	6	4	3	15	27	33
Inventory (general)	3	4	1	17	24	33
Management Reporting	4	4	2	18	28	32
Accounts Payable	9	6	3	11	28	32
Personnel	8	5	3	14	28	32
Position Control	3	6	1	17	25	32
Reporting(fin aid)	2	4	4	16	26	31

KEY

A = Number of offices voting the system "Critical"
B = Number of offices voting the system "Useful"
C = Number of offices voting "Nice to Have"
D = Number of offices votinf "Have No Need of System"
E = Number of unique offices responding
F = Percent of responding offices unhappy with the system

It is instructive to compare the Question 4 rating of value of the system with those felt to be inadequate, as illustrated in Table 9.4. The systems that are both critical and inadequate at a high rate are in bold.

WHY SHOULD WE GO CLIENT/SERVER?

We organized a task force that established goals for going to client/server improvements and identified user community goals as:

• Technological trends in client/server computing foster cost effective service.
• End users know their needs. If they are able, they will satisfy them. Overheads of cost, time, and organization become minimal. Decomposing workloads to modules in a client/server model should be effective in simplifying user involvement and decisions. Interplay in performance, configuration, and system logic lessens in those discussions and are left to the campus data processing infrastructure.
• Growth of networking has increased the cost effectiveness of distribution to work with centralized processing and storage. Stanislaus has a big investment in networking capable of being used in this way.
• Timeliness should improve by eliminating a single "bottleneck" office with multiple priorities in favor of sharing multiple nodes across offices.
• Negative sanctions of staying with the older "totally central" mainframe technology. The old mainframe solution has an increasing maintenance cost. Continuing it is financially unattractive, even punitive. Risks of catastrophic IS system losses grow with time on the older technology.

We want to identify the risks in going to this model too. Minimizing these risks will also contribute to success. We expect that the commitment to episodes of development in a client/server model will tax our institution's commitment and memory. Priorities have a way of being dynamic. It will take real wisdom to distinguish the true need for changes in priorities from those driven by politics or personalities. Also, we can not be sure the system life cycle is not shorter than the development life cycle. If we are wrong we will not complete our institution's development before the new is too old to function well. We are explicitly trusting we can achieve short development times and that technology will continue to move in the direction of client/server models or logical extensions of them.

This suggests to us a clear institutional organization and planning process, widely communicating within the entire planning process. Wide organizational appreciation of the model and goals is necessary. Also, we must follow technology with a particular eye toward changes outdating client/server models.

WHY COORDINATE INSTITUTIONAL INFORMATION?

Our task force recognized that some systems are "corporate" in nature. They affect all offices. Their usefulness depends upon coordinating among offices. Types of coordination required include:

- Synchronization of data
- Data collection responsibility
- Database administration
- Update and quality assurance
- Networking protocols and design
- Standards of programming
- Operations scheduling
- Enhancements to and maintenance of the systems
- Version control
- Access and security
- Network access security and protocols.

PRODUCTS OF THE TASK FORCE

The Task Force completed its studies, its hosting of campus visits by vendors to educate the community, and its visits to sister institutions. Its efforts culminated in several documents. We developed Issue Papers for the community on topics such as these: "Information Systems Plan to Plan," "Strategic Issues and Opportunities in Information Systems," and "Distribution versus Centralization of Information Systems." Brief papers were produced on "Information Systems Project Life Cycle," "Software Version Conflicts," "Needs Justification," and "Personality-Based Design." Most significant of these efforts were a "Campus Administrative Information Systems Master Plan," and "An Alternatives Study of Administrative Information Systems." We used them in some briefings of the university's executive administration and we anticipate approval and funding of the implementation. Defining needs and objectives may prove to be the hardest task for the community to achieve in this project.

Chapter Ten

USING THE CLIENT/SERVER PARADIGM IN COLLEGE ADMINISTRATIVE COMPUTING

Dale Nimrod
Computing Center Director
Luther College

OVERVIEW

This chapter explores aspects of the client/server approach to administrative computing in higher education. It draws on the literature and on the experience of Luther College, an institution with about 2,300 students and a modest IT staff, in the initial stages of migrating to this new technology. The chapter is intended especially for planners of administrative computing.

We offer the conclusion that the client/server technology *does* make sense for small institutions with small IT staffs. Moreover, because one of the positive characteristics of client/server architecture is its *scalability*, one can start from a modest viewpoint and legitimately scale up to a larger viewpoint or to a more general viewpoint.

On the other hand, the literature reviewed for the preparation of the chapter comes mainly from representatives of larger universities, businesses, and the computing industry, abundantly convinced of the applicability of client/server architecture for them. Many would go so far as to use the term "inevitable."

The chapter addresses the following topics:

- The concept of client/server architecture.
- The deficiencies of traditional online transaction processing in meeting administrative computing needs.
- The importance of industry standards in freeing IT organizations and developers to adopt this new paradigm.
- Managing the migration from the old paradigm to the new.
- The role of vendors of administrative software packages for higher education.
- Suggested readings.

CLIENT/SERVER COMPUTING

The client/server approach is one of cooperative computing. Although there are some very general definitions of client/server technologies, it will be instructive to consider initially an arrangement of multiple clients connected to a single server (Figure 10.1):

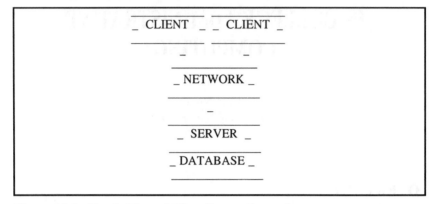

Figure 10.1   Simple View of Client/Server Computing

The client in Figure 10.1 signifies not a person, but a desktop computer running software for the end user. For instance, suppose that the software is an application program running on the client computer and that it requires data from the database computer.

The client/server technology permits the cooperation between the client and server to take place transparently. The *end user* doesn't need to know of the term "download;" the *application program* doesn't need to know how the data is stored in the database; and the *database server* somehow figures out how to transfer only the data needed across the network. Note that the client is not running a terminal emulation program, but the application program itself.

To an end user who uses a desktop computer for word processing, spreadsheet manipulations, graphics creation, and the like, potential opportunities for exploiting this arrangement come immediately to mind. The most obvious opportunity is the potential for *accessing* the institutional database from the same common (and familiar) desktop user interface. Beyond accessing the database, without help from the IT staff, desktop computer users know how to *transfer output* from a computer run into their spreadsheets, word processors, and statistical packages for subsequent manipulation. So the opportunities have only begun: end users view Figure 10.1 as one of empowerment.

To the IT organization that traditionally provides the wherewithal to access the database, some apparent opportunities also exist. Programmers appreciate the Fourth Generation Language (4GL) facilities that exist on desktop computers to generate applications programs that employ the same graphical user interface (GUI) that end users find in off-the-shelf word processors, spreadsheets, and graphics packages. For the IT staff members responsible for training, the commonality of the end user interface between these packages and the applications programs is even more important than their graphical nature. Furthermore, distribution of the computer power offers a potential way of extending the life of the host housing the database. And, finally, it appears possible to provide these things without abdicating the entrusted responsibility of managing the security and the integrity of the institutional database. Maybe the IT organization can concentrate on something more productive than trying to corral the maverick end user.

What has to be done by whom in order to make client/server computing work? Do the efforts required to make it all work together plus the efforts to migrate from a current mode of operation outweigh the advantages for the end user and the applications developer?

To answer these questions, the components making up the boxes of the client/server diagram in Figure 10.1 must be identified. Importantly, the needed ingredients are becoming available from a choice of vendors. And one can mix an ingredient providing one function from one vendor with an ingredient for another function from another vendor. So the need to develop all of the necessary ingredients in-house is not only unnecessary, but unwise.

Thanks to the concerted efforts of many in developing standards, it is possible to have things arranged such that an application program does not need to know how the data is structured in the database. Vendor-supported products are available to make this "back-door computer independence" possible. Figure 10.2 splits the CLIENT box of Figure 10.1 into three components:

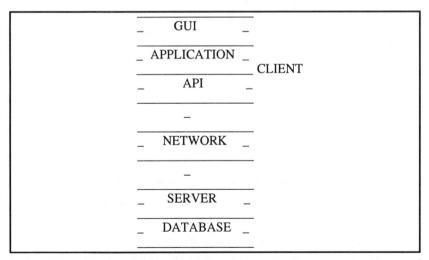

Figure 10.2   Components of the Client in a Simple View of a Client/Server System

The diagram in Figure 10.2 conveys the idea that an application program is written to "speak" to a GUI for interacting with the end user and with an API to communicate to the server across the network. Note that the application program speaks directly neither to the end user nor to the database. Much of the value of the client/server approach derives from this arrangement. The application is relieved of having to provide all the bells and whistles—pop-up windows, icons, a mouse, pull-down-menus, and scroll-bars—that desktop computer users have come to expect. Instead, the application program simply activates and feeds those features of a vendor-supported graphical user interface such as Microsoft Windows for PCs, Apple's Macintosh, X-Windows, or IBM's Presentation Manager.

The job of the vendor-supported application programming interface (API) is to translate database requests, direct them to the server, and receive and translate the replies for the application. The server may need to further translate the calls from the API to match a particular relational database management system (RDBMS), but the point is that the application program resident on the client is spared from providing the database retrieval structural specifics. Given modern 4GL-based application generators, cranking out application programs that are easily maintained appears manageable to even a modest IT organization.

Figure 10.3 shows that end users see more than applications programs from the power seat of the client/server paradigm:

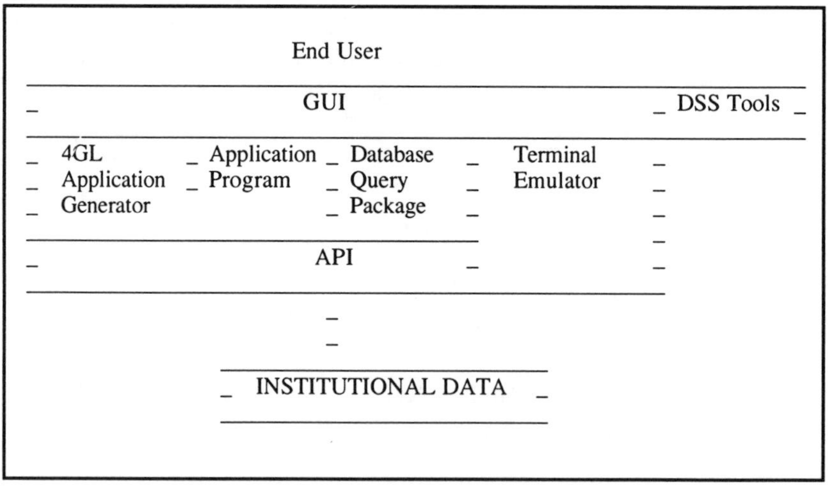

End User				
_ GUI				_ DSS Tools _
_ 4GL _ Application _ Generator	_ Application _ Program	_ Database _ Query _ Package	_ Terminal Emulator	_ _ _
_ API			_	_
_ _				
_ INSTITUTIONAL DATA _				

Figure 10.3   The Client/Server System from the End User Perspective

As has been seen, from the GUI of choice (e.g., Microsoft Windows) end users can run applications. Optionally, they can run a vendor-supported database query program. Queries can be prepared on an ad hoc basis by end users, or they (perhaps a robust set) can be prepared beforehand by the IT organization. Additional customizing of a canned query is well within the capability of most users.

A GUI-based terminal emulator is included in the mix of available facilities in case it might be needed for running server-based applications and for launching server-based batch jobs (handling the necessary remote procedure calls is not yet standardized, and hence, a terminal emulator facility might be necessary to accomplish these tasks.) The diagram also shows that the end user can reach GUI-based word processors, spreadsheets, statistical packages, and other decision support systems (DSS) through the same GUI. And since the GUI includes some kind of "clipboard" facility for cutting and pasting, the clipboard becomes the mechanism for transferring the output from an application or from a database query to, for example, a spreadsheet, word processor, or graphics package. The 4GL application generator shown in Figure 10.3 is not meant to imply that end users should be the ones to program applications. On the other hand, the diagram is meant to convey that applications programmers do their jobs using GUI at the client.

Figure 10.3 represents what the IT organization at Luther College is preparing to implement for its administrative computing users. Each of the components except the application program are vendor-supported products. A later section deals with how the migration from the current environment is being accomplished, but the reader might surmise correctly that the terminal emulator is a key tool during the migration.

Before leaving the view of the client/server from the Figure 10.3 visualization, it is useful to consider the approach of Reed College to accomplish most of the same goals for administrative computing as Luther College. Reed has judged that the set of applications programs that it purchased in an off-the-shelf higher education administrative package is adequate for accomplishing what the applications programs in Figure 10.3 are designed for. Therefore, at Reed, "application program" in Figure 10.3 disappears from the client and exists instead on the server (Figure 10.4), as they have been during the 1980s in a time-shared computing environment. But they are now being launched from the GUI through the terminal emulator shown in the figure.

Important to the success of the Reed College project was that the vendor of the administrative computing package had chosen to put the Reed database into a RDBMS for which an independent database server exists. The upshot is that Reed end users can sit at a GUI of choice (in Reed's case either a Macintosh or a PC running Microsoft Windows) and choose among the following options:

- Use the terminal emulator to run an application on the server-based computer
- Use the client-based database query facility to run fresh or canned queries
- Transfer the output from either of the above options to DSS tools.

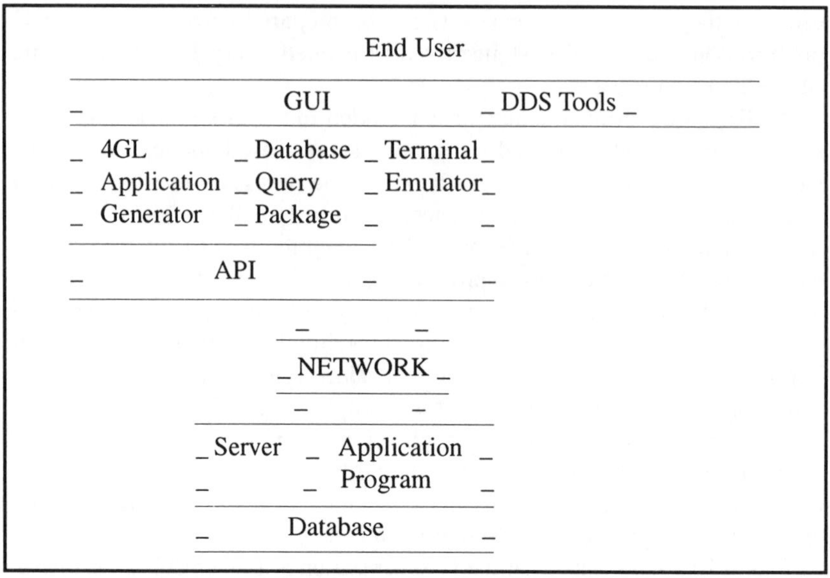

End User			
_	GUI	_ DDS Tools _	
_ 4GL _ Application _ Generator	_ Database _ Query _ Package	_ Terminal_ _ Emulator_ _	
_	API	_	_
	_	_	
	_ NETWORK _		
	_	_	
_ Server _	Application _ Program	_	
_	Database	_	

Figure 10.4   Reed College Graphical User Interface Project

Whether the Reed version of a common and graphical user interface fits everyone's definition of client/server doesn't matter, because everything the college has done is compatible with client/server architecture. If and when Reed feels it would like to start generating some applications programs to run on the client, the infrastructure to support that is in place. This situation also provides a hint as to a manageable mechanism for migrating from traditional online transaction processing to the client/server approach.

The details of what is included in Figure 10.4's "NETWORK" box are not dealt with in this chapter. It should be obvious, however, that some networking software must be running both on the client computer and on the server computer. Some authors would prefer visualizing both of them inside the "NETWORK" box; some would even like to visualize the API to be inside the "NETWORK" box instead of in the "CLIENT" box (see Figure 10.1). With this visualization, the network becomes a robust "broker" of data between the client and the server instead of simply a data communications facility.

THE FORCE DRIVING THE MOVE FROM OLTP TO CLIENT/SERVER

In contrast with much of the developments in the delivery of administrative computing over the years, technological developments that have enabled doing the same administrative functions better and faster do not seem to be the driving force of client/server. Rather, its compelling motivation is a new set of end users with different needs than former users. These influential new users are the managers of information and the decision makers—the vice presidents and department managers who have previously asked their staffs to prepare computer reports and gather information from the administrative computing system. These people have been using desktop computers for some time now for word processing, for modeling with spreadsheets, and communicating with colleagues.

Now these managers want to get their hands on institutional data, perform some analyses of their own, and look for some quantitative support for their decisions. To get to the data, they don't want to turn their friendly desktop computers into dumb terminals connected to the institutional database, with software designed to automate clerical tasks—and they will not be denied. With all of the advantages of desktop-based computing, offices are going to find a way to migrate as much as possible to their desktops, one way or another, with or without cooperation from the IT organization. Even if it requires downloading or re-entering, and maintaining duplicate data, desktop solutions are going to be used.

The challenge for the IT organization is to help these users migrate to desktop-based computing without jeopardizing the integrity and security of the shared data. The client/server technology seems to be a major key to success. At Luther College, for example, we have attempted to meet the administrative computing needs through software developed in-house (for the most part) on a traditional minicomputer. The database was migrated to a relational database system a few years ago, and the third generation programming languages have been largely supplanted with fourth generation report languages and some powerful software development tools.

But several problems faced us:

- A long list of applications were waiting to be developed
- The pressure to accommodate executive decision-support functions was growing
- Our ability to provide long-term maintenance of software developed in house worried us.

Our first attempt to overcome these problems was a study undertaken to see whether one of the off-the-shelf administrative computing packages offered by several vendors would meet our needs. With the support of the top college administrators, we composed a Request for Information (RFI) in December 1988 and sent it to over two dozen vendors. We were disappointed to discover decision support lacking in all of the responses, that maintenance requirements on our IT staff would still be high, and that the approach of all of the packages pretty much emulated our own—online transaction processing on a traditional time-shared host, and a mountain of source code. The PC-based network solutions at that time were inadequate to meet our level of expectation. We did not expect in 1989 that any respondent would report its package was built on a client/server approach, but we asked them all whether they were looking into the possibility. Not a single vendor reported that it was even thinking of that design. The responses to our RFI prompted us to abandon the search for off-the-shelf packages to solve our problems. We turned instead to working on the infrastructure that would enable us to adopt the client/server paradigm within which we would migrate our administrative computing systems. We are convinced that we made the right decision.

STANDARDS FOR COMPONENTS OF CLIENT/SERVER ARCHITECTURE

The years of work that have gone into developing standards for networking and for relational database management systems, for open standards of interoperability, as well as de facto standards, are paying off handsomely in the client/server architecture. Their acceptance is the key that enables vendors to create needed products for the architecture, and IT organizations to select pieces of the architecture from a range of choices. The reader is referred to the articles by Bernbom (1991), by Freeman and York (1991), and by White (1992), listed at the end of the chapter, for a discussion of those standards.

THE MIGRATION PROCESS

It is exceedingly difficult to swap one college-wide software system for another in one plunge. One would like to approach the task one office at a time. But if all of the offices are serviced from an integrated database, how is it possible to migrate to a client/server arrangement from one seemingly quite different a step at a time?

Fortunately, many institutions and businesses have found ways to do it successfully. At Luther College, we were able to adjust the old relational database to access tables of the new database equipped with the server. Therefore, all old applications programs continue to work, even if some of their old data has been moved to the new database. Data can therefore be moved as new applications requiring the data to be accessed through the server are developed—step by step, office by office. Such movement does not affect applications from other offices that require the same data.

Importantly, this scheme, represented in Figure 10.5, permits *moving* the data, *not copying*, to the new database. Data does not have to be stored redundantly in both databases during migration.

(The dashed line between the old and new databases is a "semi-permeable membrane," allowing data to pass from the new to the old, but not vice versa. Data is not stored redundantly in both databases.) A diagram, however, cannot adequately represent the change in thinking that must accompany the migration. Programmers can be trained to use the new tools, new interfaces, and object-oriented programming effectively, but methodologies for design and application development that IT organizations have relied on will need to be rethought.

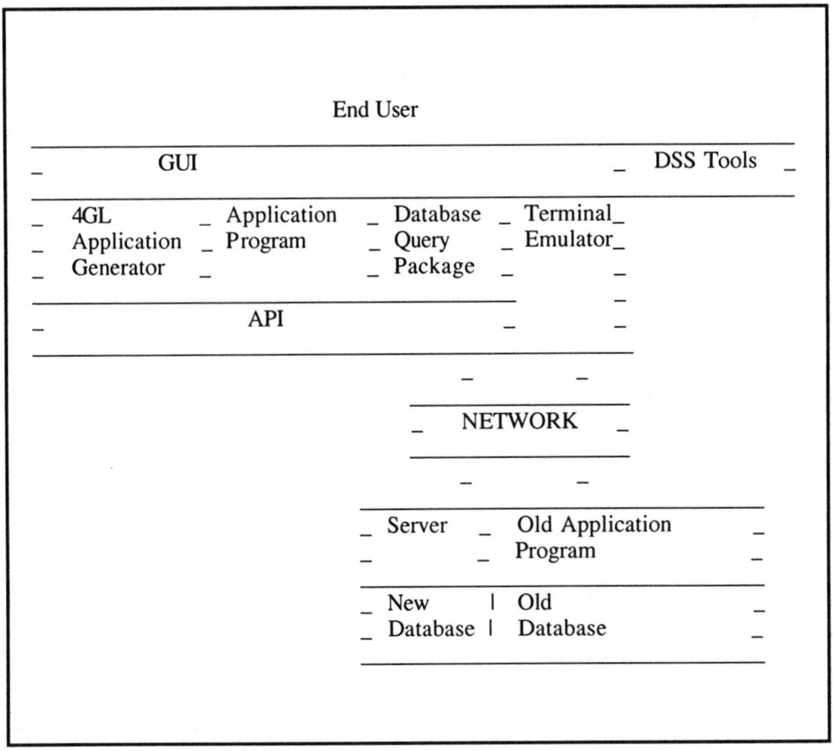

```
┌─────────────────────────────────────────────────────────────────┐
│                          End User                                 │
│  ─          GUI                                 ─   DSS Tools  ─  │
│ ─ 4GL          ─ Application  ─ Database ─ Terminal─               │
│ ─ Application  ─ Program      ─ Query    ─ Emulator─               │
│ ─ Generator    ─               ─ Package ─        ─               │
│ ─             API                          ─     ─                │
│                                        ─      ─                   │
│                              ─   NETWORK   ─                       │
│                                        ─      ─                   │
│                         ─ Server  ─ Old Application   ─           │
│                         ─          ─ Program          ─           │
│                         ─ New      │ Old              ─           │
│                         ─ Database │ Database         ─           │
└─────────────────────────────────────────────────────────────────┘
```

Figure 10.5.   Diagram of Luther College Scheme for Migrating from an Old Administrative System to Client/Server

As all good writers know, one writes for an audience and, in the 1990s, the audience for administrative computing is not the same one developers wrote for in the previous decade. The challenge to deliver to the new audience the technological wherewithal to access the institutional data from a friendly interface while preserving the security and integrity of the data is still only part of the task. In the words of one author (Wood 1992), paving the way for productive decentralized access requires making sure that the data is sufficiently "friendly." For data to be "friendly," a carefully written user guide is a necessity. The names of data elements and the care with which they are defined requires new standards.

Gaps still exist in available tools to bring to bear on the new development environment. CASE tools, which have worked well to enforce development procedures in host-based computing development, are currently sorely missed in developing client/server computing. But products and help are filling the gaps. By 1992, not only are there numerous companies selling seminars and workshops on client/server technology, but at least one is selling a workshop on managing the migration.

WHAT SHOULD THE VENDORS PROVIDE?

Throughout this chapter, we have emphasized the role of the IT organization. But at the same time, we have pointed out that "going it alone" is a foolish posture to adopt.

The products the vendors should provide fall into two categories: (1) products to plug into the client/server architecture (largely independent of higher education), and (2) products especially designed for higher education. If a vendor product is to be useful in providing a functional component of a client/server architecture, it must first and foremost meet industry standards for interoperability. Beyond that, vendors will put into the products the standard and the creative features, documentation, support, and the like that attracts buyers to the product.

The most traditional products especially geared for administrative computing in higher education are applications programs and the accompanying databases. Several vendors have been successful in providing complete packages that are integrated across the administrative units of a college or university. Most vendors of these packages have been alert in listening to user groups and responding with increasingly friendlier screens and user-controlled ad hoc reporting facilities.

This chapter concludes with the suggestion that client/server technology provides vendors of administrative computing software with some new opportunities. Some vendors, no doubt, will strive to put a fully integrated package in the client/server paradigm, but we perceive a need for quite a different type of product than has traditionally been offered.

We suggest that a receptive market might exist for a vendor-supported package, starting first with a well thought-out database designed from the vendor's experience with higher education. The vendor would structure the database in a SQL-based relational database management system for which there exists one or more vendor-supported database servers.

The vendor would add to its offering consultation in choosing network components and in choosing components for the client. And probably the vendor would want to offer the customer a chance or a source to buy a Department of Education-certified financial aid calculator module and perhaps a standard payroll package. The rest of the traditional applications might not have to be included—and if the vendor felt compelled to provide a plate of applications programs, they could be offered as unsupported modules with source code.

Given the available vendor-supported *tools* and a robust vendor-supported *database design*, many IT organizations might decide they are positioned to generate their own applications programs, customized to their own situations. Such an offering might be attractive to a vendor because the cost of supporting a database design is much less than the cost of supporting all of the applications programs and endless customer requests for enhancements and customizations. IT organizations might conclude that the staff requirements for maintaining their own applications programs in the new environment are manageable and that there might be a better place to invest the savings.

SUGGESTED READINGS

The computing industry literature has suddenly been filled with articles on client/server computing. Some of the articles that were helpful in preparing this chapter are listed below. The article by Bernbom of Indiana University and the article co-authored by Freeman of the Gartner Group and York of the University of Cincinnati are particularly recommended. Their coverage of the concept of client/server and the implications for higher education and for IT organizations within higher education is exceptionally thorough and carefully written. The paper by Ringle and Schmedding of Reed College is particularly helpful in seeing an innovative and manageable migration path to client/server computing.

Bernbom, Gerald. Data Administration and Distributed Data Processing. *CAUSE/EFFECT*: Winter 1991.

"Client/Server Computing with the SQL System," Gupta Technologies, Inc., 1990.

Freeman, Grey and Jerry York. Client/Server Architecture Promises Radical Changes. *CAUSE/EFFECT*: Spring, 1991.

Fronczak, Christine. "HP 3000 Open Systems and Client/Server Computing," Hewlett-Packard Company, 1992.

Hardcastle, King, Hargrave, and Gerik. "Moving to the Client/Server Model," CAUSE National Conference paper #CNC9137, 1991.

"How to Choose a SQL Database Server for Novell Networks and Windows Applications," Gupta Technologies, Inc., December, 1991.

Lopez, Ruben. "Is Client/Server the Future of Information Processing?," CAUSE National Conference paper #CNC9135, 1991.

Mulgaonkar, Anjali P. "HP ALLBASE/SQL PC API," Commercial Systems Division of the Hewlett-Packard Company, 1992.

Ringle, Martin and Heidi Schmedding. "The Reed Graphical Interface Project," CAUSE National Conference paper, December, 1992.

White, Colin "Database Gateways: The Impact of New Standards," DataBase Associates for Gupta Technologies, Inc., August, 1992.

Wood, Lamont. Paving the Way for End-User SQL Tools. *Datamation*: November 15, 1992.

ACKNOWLEDGEMENT

Steven J. Demuth, former Coordinator of Administrative Data Processing at Luther College, saw in 1988 that the client/server concept could be the key for expanding access to the Luther centralized database. His insight and single-handed persistence leading the rest of us to implementation is gratefully acknowledged.

Chapter Eleven

NETWORKED ADMINISTRATIVE INFORMATION SERVICES FOR NONTRADITIONAL CLIENTS AT PITTSBURG STATE UNIVERSITY

Robert Keith
Director of Information Systems
Pittsburg State University

Michael Brennan
Systems Software and Networking
Support Specialist for Information Systems
Pittsburg State University

INTRODUCTION

Pittsburg State University is a public institution under the jurisdiction of the Kansas Board of Regents. Located in the southeast corner of Kansas, Pittsburg State offers undergraduate and graduate degree programs to over 6,300 full time equivalent students.

Since 1985 Pittsburg State University, through the Office of Information Systems (OIS), has provided its faculty and staff with a number of information services designed to assist their administrative and advising activities. These services have since been incorporated in the University's campus-wide information system.

In 1986 a number of additional systems were added to provide a variety of unique services for students with department specific majors and other specialized departmental and office needs. Figure 11.1 provides a list of the services currently being offered. In 1987 the University installed an optical fiber-based, campus-wide local area network (LAN), which was implemented to expand significantly the student, faculty and staff access to University administrative and academic information. The initial implementation of this network spawned the need to establish methods for the secure and "client friendly" delivery of this information to a much broader client base, including access by students to their University information.

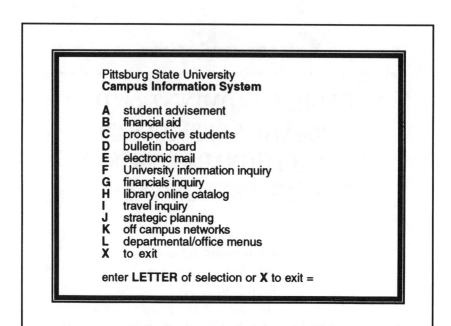

Figure 11.1 List of Information Services for Faculty and Staff

Patterned after the customer service concept of point-of-sale equipment, a 3.5-inch computer diskette was used instead of the traditional credit or debit card. This diskette, when inserted into any one of over two hundred micro-computers located on campus for student use, would initiate the service. Using this concept OIS embarked on its student "Gorilla Card," or "*GoCARD*" project. [Note: The gorilla is the official University mascot, hence the service and project name.)

The *GoCARD* project objectives were simple: (1) implement the service using a carefully defined and controlled project approach, (2) provide for ease of service access using existing networked hardware and software, (3) assure "client friendly" access by any student to his/her University information, (4) establish a networked interface between the campus-wide LAN and the University administrative computer, (5) maintain access security and student information confidentiality, and (6) keep operational support requirements and ongoing costs to a minimum.

PROJECT PHASE ONE

The first project phase defined the services that could be made available to the students. Figure 11.2 shows the services currently available, with footnotes indicating those initially offered, those added during the last four years, and those to be added in the near term. A brief summary of each service follows.

Demographic Information

A set of four screens that display a student's current University demographic information. Selected information on these screens, such as local and permanent address, may be changed by the student. Any changed information is reported daily to the Registrar's office staff for auditing.

Class Schedule

Detail of the student's current and previous three semesters' enrollment. Figure 11.3 provides a sample of the data used for this screen.

Unofficial Transcript

Provides the student with the complete transcript detail for any or all of three transcript types: undergraduate, graduate and continuing studies. The student may look at a specified semester or may browse through all transcript pages.

Bulletin Board

University-wide public information including campus activities, campus calendar, student union events, employment opportunities, situations wanted, and several categories for items and services for sale or wanted. Students, faculty, and staff may place bulletin board items at any time with an automatic two-week item display expiration.

Trial Enrollment

The ability to create a student pre-enrollment schedule including all checks for closed classes, time conflicts, instructor permission, holds, etc. The creation of this schedule, in advance of the enrollment periods, can significantly reduce the time required for student enrollment.

Unofficial Degree Audit

Using the transcript information, this function allows a student to see what courses are remaining to be taken to satisfy degree requirements given his/her current degree/major/minor combination. This information can also be used as a "what if" modeling tool for other degree/major combinations of interest to the student.

Accounts Receivable Inquiry

Shows the balances and the detail included in the balances for all of the student's accounts receivable items.

Financial Aid Status

The current status of the student's financial aid application(s) and funds disbursement.

Electronic Mail

Electronic mail may be sent and received from other students, faculty, and staff.

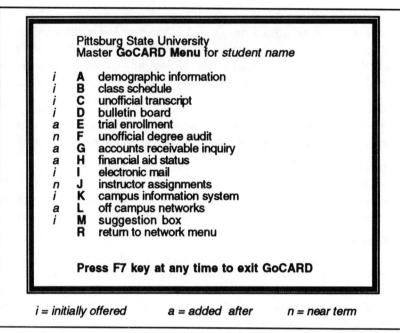

Figure 11.2 Information Services for Students

Student schedule inquiry as of **12/01/92** for term **92/WF** 1 of 2

RYAN S STUDENT 1234567 class **2** cred att **43.50** A/R $ **0.00**

cur hours **14.50** cum GPA **3.541** advisor **ADVISOR NAME**

major **MUSIC** degree **BA**

local address **100 MAIN** local phone **555-8888**
ANYWHERE, KS 49888

PSYCH*155*01	GEN PSYCH	3.00	08:30-09:20AM	MWF
INSTRUCTOR NAME				HH214
ENGL*103*01	ENG COMP	3.00	09:30-10:20AM	MWF
INSTRUCTOR NAME				GH301
PHYSICS*175*02	DES ASTRONOMY	3.00	12:30-01:20PM	MWF
INSTRUCTOR NAME				YH102
MATH*113*08	COLLEGE ALG	3.00	06:30-09:20PM	M
INSTRUCTOR NAME				YH215

enter **N** next page or **X** to exit =

BOLD = bold white *italic* = cyan ----- = bold green
screen prompt = bold yellow on red single keystroke entry

Figure 11.3 Sample *GoCard* Screen

Instructor Assignments

On a paperless basis, the instructor may assign class work, the student may respond to that assignment, and the faculty member may, in turn, provide comments and or grading related to the student's work.

Campus Information System

Primarily a text retrieval system with key word searching and a master index. Text documents available for searching include class schedules, the University catalog, the student handbook, and a variety of current news-based documents published by University departments and offices.

Off Campus Networks

Access to KANREN (KANsas Research and Education Network) for the use of Regent university libraries and other selected statewide, national, and international electronic information services.

Suggestion Box

Student suggestions for new services, current service enhancements, or problem description.

REMAINING PHASES

During the completion of this project phase, OIS contacted each administrative office that had primary responsibility for the data that would be used for each information service. This process involved explaining in detail the objectives of the student *GoCARD* services, how they would be offered, the benefits of making this information available to students, and the methods that would be used for maintaining security and confidentiality. Gaining these approvals from each office involved was a mission critical step. The University Registrar, Controller, Director of Enrollment Management, and student services staff were the main contact points for this project phase and, after the project details were presented, all of these offices agreed totally with the service offerings.

The second phase of the project involved the establishment of service standards and identifying the source of the information to be used. The definition of the service standards centered around the "client friendly" project objective. Defined standards included the use of color in screen presentation, system messaging, menuing and menu selection, screen layout, subroutines for information retrieval, the physical *GoCARD* diskette design, and security features and physical network utilization (detailed later in this chapter). Since OIS had gained a great deal of experience using a common database management system adopted in 1981 for all of its administrative systems, the task of identifying information sources and access standards was quite straightforward.

The third project phase involved the completion of a prototype system that would be used as the basis for the initial product offering.

The fourth project phase involved offering the *GoCARD* prototype to a carefully selected student group. Freshmen through graduate level students were chosen from course enrollments on a random basis. Members of the University student governing body were also added, bringing the total test group to about four hundred and fifty. *GoCARD* diskettes were issued to this test group, and testing of the prototype system was conducted for six months. During the six-month period detailed surveying was completed for the test group. The results showed that surprisingly few service modifications were required.

REALIZATION OF PROJECT OBJECTIVES

Our controlled approach to implementation allowed us to realize the remaining five project objectives listed on page 106. Each of these is described more fully in the following sections.

Ease of Service Access

The *GoCARD* service is accessed through the use of a personalized 3.5-inch diskette provided to the student following the successful completion of the application process. A *GoCARD* application is one of the services available on the general University LAN. The *GoCARD* diskette may then be used in any of the University's networked PC-compatible microcomputers. All of the services available are accessed using single key selections via menus. The service also makes extensive use of color and highlighting in screen displays to guide the student quickly to the required information. Figure 11.3 provides an example of the single keystroke approach and the color schemes used to highlight service information.

Access by Any Student to His/Her University Information

The uniqueness of the *GoCARD* service is based on students' ability to view their own University information. Since all of the University's administrative

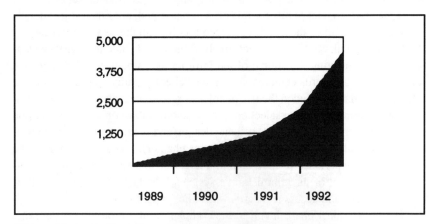

Figure 11.4 *GoCards* Issued

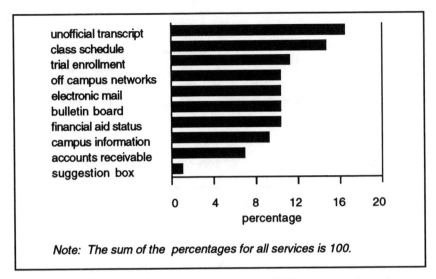

Figure 11.5   *GoCard* Services Use Percentage, 1992

applications are online, with information updates performed in real time, users can obtain current information. For example, the Registrar Office staff may be in the process of capturing end-of-semester grade results from course rosters. At the same time a student, using his/her *GoCARD* diskette, may be viewing current course enrollment information. The first view by the student may show no grade information at all, but seconds later another view may show the grade results of one or more courses taken. Obviously, during enrollment and at the end of the semester, *GoCARD* activity is very high. Figure 11.4 shows the history of *GoCARD* issuance in terms of number of cards and Figure 11.5 shows the current percentage breakdown of the services used.

Establish a Networked Interface

The *GoCARD* services currently operate by means of an asynchronous interface between the University LAN and the administrative computing system. A pool of RS-232C lines connects the UNIX LAN servers to the administrative computer (see Figure 11.6). An asynchronous server package runs on the UNIX servers and manages the servers' serial ports. Client-based communications software supports the client/server interaction.*

---

* A project is currently underway to replace the asynchronous connectivity with a TCP/IP ethernet link. This project is being undertaken to allow a higher speed interface and to provide support for the tremendous growth currently being experienced with other networked sharing of the administrative data. Additionally, the current administrative system is being replaced with UNIX-based RISC processors to effect significant administrative computing cost reductions.

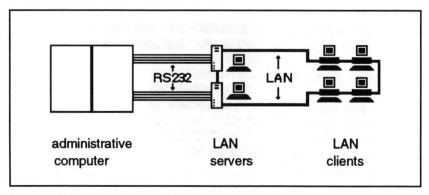

administrative   LAN   LAN

computer   servers   clients

Figure 11.6   *GoCard* Network Schematic

The *GoCARD* activated client PC workstation requests the administrative computer connection through the LAN server, and the administrative computer software, developed by OIS staff, then supports the subsequent session. For the student client, establishing the connection and breaking the connection are simply completed by the use of a single key stroke.

The student, using a PC-compatible workstation, initiates a *GoCARD* session with a single key selection. The session setup is handled automatically by a combination of OIS-developed and off-the-shelf software. The detailed steps of establishing connectivity consist of:

1. The student selects *GoCARD* from the LAN network menu, which invokes custom *GoCARD* software executing on the PC client.
2. The student is prompted to insert the *GoCARD* diskette in the PC diskette drive.
3. The software verifies the *GoCARD* authenticity by checking the disk format and calculating checksums.
4. The software retrieves encrypted *GoCARD* diskette information, updates counter fields, and invokes the communication package to initiate the administrative computer connection.
5. Under script control, the communications package places a network request for an asynchronous server port.
6. The communications package performs an information exchange and handshaking with the OIS custom developed administrative computer *GoCARD* software.
7. The communications package turns control to the student client, who then directly interacts with the administrative computer *GoCARD* software.
8. The administrative computer prompts for a four-digit personal identification number (PIN) [discussed in detail later in the chapter].

9. The administrative computer presents the student client with the personalized *GoCARD* menu (Figure 11.2).

Although a number of steps are involved in establishing connectivity, the average connect period is approximately eight seconds. This current "low tech" solution has been remarkably responsive and flexible since its inception more than four years ago.

Maintain Access Security and Confidentiality

The 3.5-inch *GoCARD* diskette is primarily responsible for student identification. In use, as was mentioned earlier, it functions as a medium similar to that of a magnetically encoded credit card used extensively in a variety of point-of-sale devices and automated teller machines. No executable software resides on the *GoCARD* diskette: all client software is served over the LAN. The *GoCARD* diskette must remain inserted in the PC client at all times during a session. In the event it is removed, the system ends the session and returns the client automatically to the LAN menu.

Security and confidentiality depend on the physical integrity of the *GoCARD* diskette and the reliable identification of the diskette holder to the *GoCARD* software, which executes on the administrative computer. Physical integrity is defined as an authentic diskette being used for the *GoCARD* services and not one that is locally reproduced or copied. A certain amount of copy protection is achieved by using a nonstandard disk format on selected tracks. This format also assists in authentication because the PC client *GoCARD* software selectively examines the disk format.

OIS has developed a highly successful copy protection scheme that utilizes a special counter written to the *GoCARD* diskette. This counter is incremented with each execution of the PC client software regardless of the success of the administrative computer connection. The PC client counter is passed to the administrative computer at every successful connection and is recorded in that computer's client database. The administrative computer compares the currently passed counter with the most previous counter. The current counter value must be greater or the connection is disallowed and the client's account is disabled. A manual procedure has been developed to allow students to reinstate their *GoCARD* services by contacting OIS. This protection scheme allows quick detection of an attempt to use a duplicated card.

All client identification information is encrypted and written to diskette sectors not accessible to the DOS file system. Checksums are used as an additional authentication measure. The result is that the software can verify the authenticity of a *GoCARD* prior to establishing the administrative computer connection.

During the connection process the PC client software extracts the encrypted information from the diskette and passes that information to the administrative computer. The encrypted information includes a client identifier, a password, and the counter previously described. This handshaking process is transparent to the student client. The administrative computer software decrypts the information, identifies the client, and prompts the client to enter a four-digit PIN.

The PIN is assigned to the client during the initial diskette issuance process and may be attempted a maximum of three times before the system returns the user to the LAN menu. If the PIN has been missed excessively over several session attempts, the *GoCARD* account is disabled and the student must contact OIS for card reinstatement.

Keep Support Requirements and Costs to a Minimum

In anticipation of the success of the *GoCARD* service, the operational procedures and service administration were designed with efficiency in mind. Figure 11.7 depicts the operational work flow of the service from diskette application to diskette issuance, then to problem resolution. The *GoCARD* diskette costs the student $3.00, the break-even amount for the diskette, the pre-printed diskette logo, and the PC card issuance and tracking equipment. No attempt has been made to recoup the costs associated with use of both the LAN workstations and the administrative computer, since these costs are necessary for the continuing operation of the University's campus-wide information systems services.

FOLLOW-UP

As evidenced by the *GoCARD* issuance history depicted in Figure 11.4, this project has tremendous appeal to University students. It has provided a much simplified information access that, in turn, has significantly reduced the amount of student contact required for University administrative and departmental offices. Currently, planning being completed by the University student governing body will require a *GoCARD* for all students at no cost to the student.

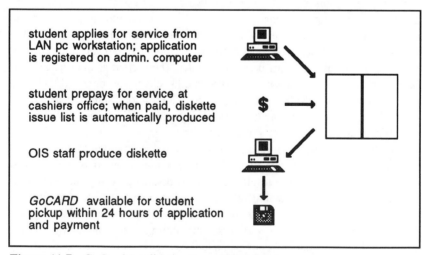

Figure 11.7 *GoCard* Application/Issue Process

Following the successful implementation of the *GoCARD* project, OIS expanded the concept of nontraditional access to University information in 1990 by planning and implementing the PSU-LINK (Pittsburg State University onLine Information NetworK) project. This project's objectives are similar to *GoCARD*, except that the client base consists of University customers remote to the campus. This group currently includes administrators and students of area high schools, community colleges, public libraries, faculty, and, soon to be added, alumni. Similar to *GoCARD*, the client workstation is either a PC-compatible or Macintosh microcomputer connecting to the University via a modem. The connectivity to the University's modem pool is completed through the use of a PSU-LINK diskette. The user issues a single command to initiate a session. Many of the same services available for *GoCARD* are also provided for PSU-LINK. A campus-based PSU-LINK coordinator has developed a comprehensive user manual and supports ongoing installation and service use training for the client base.

Chapter Twelve

ADMINISTRATIVE INFORMATION ACCESS

George J. Sullivan
Executive Associate to the Vice President for Computing
Rutgers University

INTRODUCTION

Rutgers University is the State University of New Jersey. Established in 1766, it is located primarily in New Brunswick, which has five main campuses. Two other campuses are located in Newark and Camden. Rutgers University has a student body of approximately 48,000, a staff of 5,000, and a faculty of 2,500. In 1989, Rutgers Computing Services began an intensive study of distributed computing and client/server architecture for use in administrative applications. To that end, a database committee was formed, with the author appointed the Chair of that committee.

This chapter originated as one of several "vision" statements for a self-study of Computing Services in 1991. This vision has gone through some transition as shaped by technological capabilities and institution priorities. It should be viewed as a quasi-ideological model rather than a specific road map for future directions at Rutgers. It has been edited to reflect activities through April, 1994.

This chapter defines a model for development of improved administrative information access. Some background information and history are discussed, current activities and recent offerings described, and a phased approach to data access for the future proposed.

HISTORY OF ACCESS TO ADMINISTRATIVE DATA

Administrative computer systems have been employed in universities since the late fifties. In order to explore the future of access to administrative data, it is helpful to review the background of the evolution of those systems.

Traditional Centralist Model: Early Sixties Through 1979

As in most corporate environments, early administrative computer systems were based on some form of central facility processing data in large batches (commonly called "batch processing"), eventually producing printed reports. Data was recorded by application areas on "input forms" and forwarded to the central facility for data entry into the computer. The computer stored that data in files, and central programming departments created computer application systems to process the data.

An alternate approach to batch processing developed gradually over this period. Database management systems were used to store data in large indexed databases, with access to entry, update, and inspection of data items by application area users made possible through computer terminals. At Rutgers, the database management system used was IBM's Information Management System (IMS). These "online" applications were within the purview of central programming departments only and generally contained a fair amount of batch processing and reporting components.

In general, application areas "owned" the data and little sharing between areas was encouraged, or even possible. Data was often redundant and in various nonstandard formats. Access to the data was controlled by the physical environment; only the computer department staff had access to the machine-readable data in its raw form. Users in application areas saw data only as printed reports or online terminal display.

Applications were designed for the needs of central administrative departments such as Admissions, Registration, Accounting, etc. The role of the central computer staff was to support computer operations and to perform applications development or maintenance. Needs of end-user areas were secondary (or ignored) in the design of applications. Very little direct end-user usage was supported and access to central data by end users was generally prohibited.

"User Friendly" Concept: Early Eighties

It was about this time that the computer industry realized that central computers and central programming departments would never keep pace with the exponentially growing needs of the organization for access to information. Users were encouraged to help themselves by direct access to data employing "user friendly" tools. A way around the bottleneck of central computer departments was offered to those areas willing to invest their own resources in information systems.

Although Rutgers had experienced considerable success with implementation of online applications and a dynamic increase in the terminal network, central systems were unable to meet the myriad demand from end users. As a partial remedy, Administrative Computing Services acquired MARK IV, a form-driven programming language designed for ease of use and especially suited for end users. Account-specific access software allowed selective access to production data for approved clients. A central security officer was hired to oversee and establish access rules to data and to insure that appropriate sign-offs were obtained from application area "data owners." Network Control/Help Desk staff were put in place for end-user support. Security standards were established under advisement with university auditors and enforced by the Administrative Computing Services security officer.

This approach gained some initial acceptance as users began to work directly with data and produce their own reports. Although MARK IV was much easier to use than traditional programming languages, it nonetheless required a considerable investment in time to learn. Also, users were required to learn the additional complexities of Job Control Language and the terminal monitor, TSO/ISPF. As a result, though MARK IV became a popular tool for the Administrative Computing Services programming staff, many users who were trained never developed into MARK IV programmers. To a great extent, from the end-user viewpoint, this effort met with limited success.

Personal Computers: Mid-Eighties

The advent of the personal computer sparked a resurgence in interest in direct access to central administrative data. If central data could be transferred to personal computers, truly "friendly" tools could be employed to manipulate and report on that data. Widespread acceptance of personal computer word processors, spreadsheet programs, and database systems greatly expanded the computer literate population at the typical university. Rather than enter all information locally, end users needed direct access to data from central files and databases. The complexities of mainframe programming were being replaced by the relative ease of use of the personal computer.

At Rutgers, Administrative Computing Services supported the early use of personal computers by establishing a team to help users configure, install, and resolve problems with personal computers. This team eventually became the Information Center, specializing in PC consulting and administrative PC user training. To facilitate direct access to mainframe administrative data, PC file transfer software was installed on the administrative mainframe. PC local area networks with file-sharing capabilities were also supported. Personal computer education was recruited commercially or taught directly by Information Center staff.

Even though it was now possible to manipulate data on personal computers rather easily, the task of selecting data from mainframe application systems was formidable. An end user needed to access the mainframe to gather data into a file prior to downloading to the personal computer. At Rutgers, this required a knowledge of MARK IV, which remained a cumbersome process. An alternative was to request that the file be created by central programming staff—but those requests diverted that staff from the priorities of other central application area needs. Although the staff programmers fulfilled most of these requests, the demand exceeded available resources and end users generally became frustrated with the extended time required to obtain files created for them by central staff..

Rutgers also tested another alternative during this period. An online, ad hoc query tool was acquired to allow direct access to online databases. Results of queries could be used to produce reports, to display at user terminals, or to create subfiles suitable for downloading into personal computers. The tool was Query DL/I for IMS databases. Unfortunately, IMS is not particularly efficient for ad hoc queries. It was determined that Query DL/I would not satisfy user needs without serious cost in central computer resources. Moreover, IBM had announced that it would not continue to support Query DL/I as a product.

RECENT OFFERINGS AND ACTIVITIES AT RUTGERS: 1990 - CURRENT

Within the past four years, new services have been provided on the administrative computer that have begun to more directly address users' needs. Also, a considerable amount of research has been completed in the quest for a distributed data model for the University.

New Services

With the acquisition of the new Human Resources System in 1989, Computing Services acquired IBM's DB2, a fully relational database management system. Consistent with trends in the computer industry, new systems acquired or internally developed use relational databases wherever possible. The advantage to this relational direction for administrative users is that it allows use of a more flexible query tool, the Query Management Facility, to access DB2 databases. DB2, QMF, and new offerings in OS/2 for the personal computer are part of a family of IBM products designed to improve access to data stored in a distributed network. Computing Services has also given serious consideration to the adoption of ORACLE as a suitable relational database management system for the UNIX platform. All of these tools use SQL, the Structured Query Language, which is the de facto standard for data access between computers of all sizes, brands, and technical platforms.

Electronic Mail was introduced in 1990 using facilities of TSO/ISPF and a system from UCLA (BEN). This system supports panel-driven, user-friendly electronic mail with connections to intra-University and external (Bitnet, Internet) users. Moreover, it supports a limited file transfer capability between electronic mail users. This file transfer enhances data access by allowing users to send a copy to other users of data who do not have direct access. The procedure is initiated by the sender with legitimate access to such data. Other nonmainframe-based electronic mail systems in use include Microsoft Mail, Pegasus (Novell), and MM (UNIX).

The administrative terminal network employs a proprietary IBM communications protocol, Systems Network Architecture. The standard terminal supported in this network is the IBM 3270 or equivalent. Physical connections are via dedicated telephone lines and modems. By contrast, the main university network (RUNet) uses broadband and fiber optic media to deliver high speed communications via TCP/IP, Ethernet, and DECnet protocols.

TCP/IP support was added to the administrative mainframe in early 1991, allowing a connection of administrative users to RUNet and the Internet. Initially installed for outbound communications only, this connection opened the administrative network user to the facilities of academic computing on campus and other facilities at other remote institutions. It also supports a robust file transfer capability that transcends proprietary vendor platforms.

Quite naturally, considerable concern arose about security and the potential in-bound access to the administrative computer via RUNet and the Internet. In the summer of 1992, Computing Services strengthened the RUNet connection with the implementation of non-reusable passwords. Users carry "smartcard" devices that generate random passwords. If these passwords are detected by a would-be hacker, they are unusable in subsequent logon attempts. Computing Services now supports RUNet and Internet users with access inbound to the administrative computer.

Research

Since 1989, Computing Services has been studying ways to improve access to administrative data. Several technical committees reviewed systems of various complexities and functionality. Two classes of products emerged as reasonable solutions to the current data access deficiencies.

One product class has as its function a friendly interface to the downloading of data from a mainframe to personal computer. A product in this class should allow a personal computer user to access a mainframe, select data to be downloaded regardless of its structure, and convert the downloaded data to common personal computer application formats, i.e., DIF, Lotus, dBase, WordPerfect, etc. To that end, the committee has reviewed Host Data Base View and OS/2 from IBM. Other vendor offerings that were investigated included Answer/DB (Sterling Software) and the Data Access Language, DAL, from Apple Systems.

A second class of products under study support full client/server access to data in a distributed database environment. Systems being investigated include DB2, ORACLE, CINCOM, INGRESS, and SYBASE. These products share some common elements. They are relational database systems using, or supporting, the Structured Query Language. They support, or will support, transparent access to data between applications on networked computers of any size. These systems allow users of personal workstations to access data located anywhere in the organization, in a seamless, friendly manner. Computing Services sees this as the ultimate model for user access to administrative data.

FUTURE DIRECTIONS AT RUTGERS

Future access to administrative data will be improved dramatically with the deployment of new data strategies and tools now under investigation by Computing Services. At this time, however, products designed for full distributed data access lack functionality or are overly complex. These products will no doubt improve. In the meantime, it seems reasonable to implement a phased approach to address current needs. These phases are discussed below.

Certain philosophies are expected to prevail during all phases of implementation. Access to data will be supported through the existing administrative terminals (IBM 3270 or compatible), the administrative network, and the Rutgers University Network (RUNet). The use of personal computers and workstations will be strongly recommended to replace current terminals. And, as it becomes more pervasive, there will be a shift toward RUNet as the network of choice. The security and integrity of administrative data will continue to enjoy strong emphasis as dictated by good business practice, University auditing, and federal law. Nonetheless, we must be mindful of the need to balance data protection requirements and data utility.

The design of administrative applications will shift emphasis toward meeting end users' needs as well as central administrative departments. Improved data access to central files from personal computers and departmental workstations will place increased demands on systems to provide functionality and flexibility for users. Moreover, applications will be developed or acquired that only operate on departmental workstations and personal computers. Using true client/server technologies, these applications may use mainframes as data servers *only*. The goal of the mainframe systems and the networks will be to provide seamless, transparent, any-to-any access to administrative data.

Phase I: Improve Data Distribution

During the first phase (Figure 12.1), Computing Services should select and install data distribution software for the administrative mainframe. This choice should simplify the current process of mainframe data selection, mainframe to PC downloading, and the conversion to a standard format for personal computer applications. The software employed must be user friendly, primarily PC-based, and not require the end user to be at all conversant with mainframe technologies. Answer/DB, Data Access Language Server, and OS/2 Data/Communications Managers are examples of such data distribution software.

During this phase, the mainframe application is still considered the source for authoritative University data. Central applications are responsible for maintenance of that data through traditional methods of terminal transaction processing, data entry, and/or optical scanning. Where practical, end-user data uploaded to the mainframe from personal computer applications may also be a source for authoritative administrative data. Data downloaded from central files will be distributed as a static point-in-time copy of those items. The

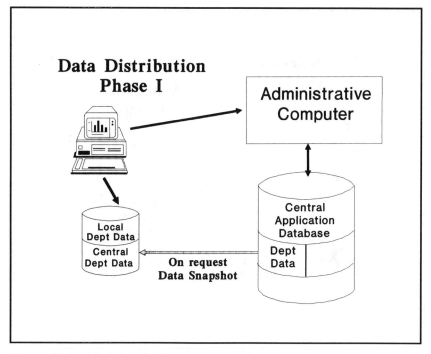

Figure 12.1   Administrative Data Access—Phase I

intention here is to avoid duplication of entry by the end-user when data already exists at the mainframe.

[Note: This phase began at Rutgers in September 1991, with a study of over fifteen vendor products. Four of these products were demonstrated to approximately sixty end users. In May, 1992, Rutgers selected Sterling Software's Answer/DB to improve data distribution and downloading. After an intensive implementation and testing effort, end users were provided limited availability to this facility in early 1993. The success of this phase has been significantly overshadowed by new developments and offerings in full client/server technologies. As a result, Computing Services will limit the employment of this Phase I product and concentrate on Phase II technologies described below.]

Phase II: Client/Server

The second phase of improving access to administrative data will require the addition of distributed database software for the mainframe, intermediate servers, and personal computers (Figure 12.2). Generally speaking, the Structured Query Language is used by most products in this class to interconnect computers and software platforms in a nearly vendor-independent manner. Access to data from computer to computer is transparent to the user, and data can be easily ported in any direction. Users are presented with a log-

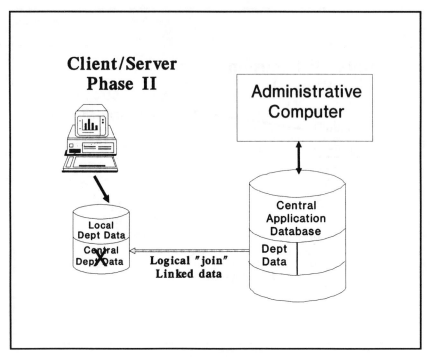

Figure 12.2 Administrative Data Access—Phase II

ical data "view" allowing a "join" of data fields regardless of where that data resides. Data distribution software acquired in Phase I may still be supported in some limited applications.

During Phase II, the authoritative source of University data is still at the central computer. Legacy mainframe applications will continue to be supported, and update of central files from other computers will continue to be restricted. Administrative data will be periodically "cloned" to "search-only" databases, which become the initial data repositories for client/server access. The intention of this phase is to further simplify administrative data access by allowing data to be located anywhere in the University network. Through client/server technologies, end users will access data logically as if it were on the users' own computer.

Similar or perhaps the same technologies will benefit the academic users of distributed data (e.g., census and full-text). Added or modified data will be available instantly from central authoritative databases. Wherever practical, new centrally programmed applications will be designed to operate fully, or in part, on personal computers and workstations in user areas.

Terminal access will continue to be supported through the administrative network, but all new connections will be handled by the RUNet. Users will be strongly encouraged to use personal computers and workstations instead of terminals. Where possible, conversion of the administrative network to RUNet will be performed.

[Note: This phase began in late 1992 with the establishment of a Future Technologies Task Force. Recommendations from this task force, published in March, 1993, have become the basis for several pilot projects employing client/server technologies for read access to administrative data. A cloned student records database was ported to an Oracle database on a UNIX server. Oracle PC client tools have been employed to demonstrate these capabilities to upper management, administrative departments, and end users. Implementation of this phase, with availability to end users, should occur by the end of 1994.]

Phase III: Distributed Database

Phase III (Figure 12.3) continues to utilize client/server distributed database software acquired in Phase II. Software offerings should be sophisticated and capable of dealing with true distributed data structures. In this model, data can be placed closer to the originating, or most used, application area (for example, perhaps the registrar's office, the School of Business, or a remote campus location). The authoritative source of data can now shift, as appropriate, to departmental systems. To serve the need for a central data repository and as a protection

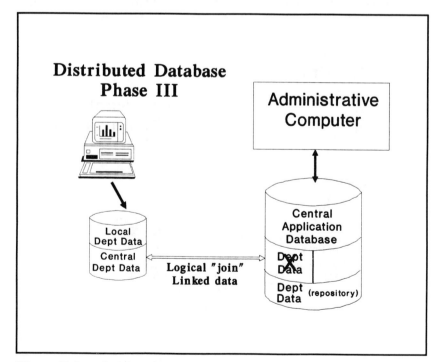

Figure 12.3 Administrative Data Access—Phase III

against failure, data redundancy will be supported centrally. Departmental data will be uploaded to intermediate servers and/or the central processor.

Access to data under a pure distributed database structure requires peer-to-peer computer connections via a high-speed communications network. Participants in this phase will be required to use the RUNet instead of the administrative network. If not already accomplished by this time, all users will be converted to RUNet for communications, and to personal computers or workstations.

Phase IV: (Future): Global University Database

In this final phase of improved data access, University data will be spread over many departmental computers and workstations, each having primary responsibility for the authority and integrity of its portion of the "global" database (Figure 12.4). Confidence in the technologies used in Phase III will facilitate a reduction in the use of central mainframe computers except as large-scale compute or database servers. The requirement for a central repository of all University data will be evaluated. As with Phase III, access to administrative data will be via RUNet only. At this stage, the network becomes the "mainframe" conceptually, as clients and servers are logically connected to perform individual tasks. Users retrieving data from the global database will be unaware of the complex data structure supporting their view of data. Data updated or added will be available everywhere instantly. The need for data redundancy will

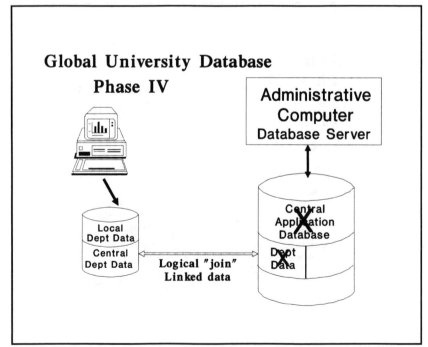

Figure 12.4   Administrative Data Access—Phase IV

be eliminated except where necessary for system performance or security.

A global distributed database structure permits all users to access data wherever it is and to use local tools to process that data. In addition to data access, the network will provide access to applications and software tools located on other computers throughout the network. The requirement for large central mainframes will be eliminated and processing of data will be accomplished on high-speed personal computers, workstations, and departmental servers. Development of system-wide policies for information control, integrity, and protection will be necessary, with corresponding requirements of responsibility and accountability.

Applications development will be handled by central or departmental teams as needed, but the applications will be localized to meet the needs of the end-user departments more completely. Transparent network access to data, applications, and computer tools will bring enormous functionality and productivity to the desktop of the future.

Chapter Thirteen

DISTRIBUTING THE POWER TO THE USERS

Ray Grant
Associate Director, Administrative Computing
Southern Oregon State College

BACKGROUND

Southern Oregon State College is a regional liberal arts institution that enrolls 4,500 students each quarter. It is located in Ashland in southwestern Oregon and provides educational services to a seven-county region. It is part of the Oregon State System of Higher Education. In the mid-1970s, the college purchased a new student information system that ran on a Honeywell Bull mainframe located 200 miles to the north. It was a batch Cobol system that was centrally maintained to serve four schools in the state.

By 1985, the student information system had been modified extensively and was difficult and expensive to maintain. A search began for a more suitable package. SOSC was given permission to acquire hardware and software and control was decentralized. In early 1989, the college purchased the Banner Student Information System from Systems and Computer Technology.

The implementation project was to last a year. This included taking delivery of a new computer, as well as Oracle database software and the Banner applications package. We also had to create new staff positions and recruit people. Users and technical staff had to be trained. New procedures were needed and data had to be converted, all within a year. We had our work cut out for us.

THE PROBLEM

The purchased package was written using Oracle database management software. With Oracle tools, the database is not difficult to manage. It is, however, a large database with many tables. Most of the purchased software consists of Oracle forms, which are used to update and query the data. The batch processes were written using SQL*REPORT, a procedural programming language that uses SQL to access the database. We planned to implement the new system as it arrived with as few changes as possible. This would make it easier to install software upgrades when they arrived. As we got into the project, though, it became clear that we would have to add some programs. In particular, the acquired package provided too few reports to support the needs of the college.

We recognized from the beginning that we did not have enough staff in Computing Services to meet the demand for specialized programming. We planned to be "live" in a year and would barely have enough time to be ready with the baseline system. There were not enough people to develop a substantial number of new reports in the time that was available. It was a frustrating experience for the programming staff and the users. We had to find a way to develop customized management information in a short period of time and with a limited staff.

ALTERNATIVES CONSIDERED

Initially, we tried to write all the programs that were needed using either SQL*PLUS or SQL*REPORT, the two Oracle languages that we had purchased. SQL*PLUS is easy to use, but not suitable for large or complex reports. SQL*REPORT is better for large reports, but it is more difficult to use.

We knew that the best approach would have been to find a good end-user tool that would allow easy access to the data for ad hoc reports. We evaluated third party software, but our effort was half-hearted. We knew we couldn't squeeze money out of the administration to buy additional software. We had already spent a lot of money on hardware, software, and staff. Upper management would not have reacted kindly to the argument that what we bought was insufficient for our needs.

Our last alternative was for the computing staff to train several users in EASY*SQL, another Oracle product. The college already had an EASY*SQL license. Perhaps users could write their own database queries. I was not crazy about this option. My concern was that users would write inefficient code and would still bother us for help. I was also not sure if they could learn how to be programmers. They were, of course, only users, not computer professionals. The word from other Banner customers was that EASY*SQL was not as easy as it promised to be.

ALTERNATIVE SELECTED

Out of desperation we decided to try to train a select group of eight users in EASY*SQL. The eight users were those who we felt had an interest in, and an aptitude for, the task. We would have to work closely with them during the training and later to support their activities. It was important to select people who could work successfully with the Computing Services staff.

Ron Wiegel, our database administrator, was the most familiar with EASY*SQL and he volunteered to teach the first course. He felt that we should first teach the basics of SQL queries using SQL*PLUS. By understanding simple queries, they could better use EASY*SQL. So, the course was designed to begin with an explanation of the *SELECT* command and relational database concepts.

TRAINING AND SUPPORT

The users were excited. Soon they would be able to get their own information without having to call computing services. The class had five people from the Business Services Office, working in the student billing and cashiering areas. They were frustrated by the lack of reports in Banner. They needed summary counts and totals to balance accounts on a daily and monthly basis. The class also had two people from the Registrar's Office and one from the Financial Aid Office.

We taught them not only how to use the *SELECT* command, but also the structure of their database. They had to know the table names and column names. We provided a complete data element dictionary for their part of the database and documentation about table keys and indexes.

Each class session involved an instructor at the front of the room and an assistant who roamed among the students to answer questions. To my surprise, the students learned the concepts quickly. The syntax of the SQL commands is not difficult and the users understood their data very well. It was easy for them to think of the data as organized in individual tables instead of associated with particular screens or Oracle forms. The students were also taught to join tables to get commonly used information, such as account balances and registration counts.

Finally, it was time to begin EASY*SQL training. Soon after the instructor began talking about EASY*SQL, it became apparent to us that the class participants were losing interest and were tapping on the keyboards. A stroll around the room confirmed my suspicion. They were busy writing queries using SQL*PLUS. They didn't want to use EASY*SQL, which required more effort to construct a single query. They were hooked on SQL*PLUS.

The EASY*SQL part of the course was abandoned. The remainder of the time was spent explaining advanced joins and report formatting. Additional exercises were given to hone the students' new skills. Oracle and database documentation was handed out and the students were told to call Computing Services if they needed help with SQL programming. System resources would be monitored and, if excessive CPU time was being used, programming help would be offered.

A second course was offered a few weeks after the initial training session. The goal was to review important concepts and teach advanced techniques. In addition, students were encouraged to share their programming success with their fellow users. It was at this class that we discovered who the real power

SQL users were going to be. The two people from the Registrar's Office didn't attend the second class because they had a programmer in their office who would provide most of their queries for them. The Financial Aid person was very interested in the class, but her needs for student system data were small because the financial aid system ran on a LAN in her office. The people from Business Services wound up writing many queries. Before the class they had trouble getting reports and totals to allow them to balance, reconcile, and do all that they had to do to make the auditors happy. Now they had as much power to look at their data as we had. They were very pleased.

PROBLEMS

Database security became an area of concern. The users were trained to use only the *SELECT* command, which will not alter the data. Once a person logs into Oracle with SQL*PLUS it is easy to experiment with commands such as *DELETE, UPDATE,* and (shudder!) *DROP.* We discovered a feature in Oracle where a profile can be defined for each user that determines exactly which commands are valid. For our population of new query users, their profiles included only the *SELECT* command. Any other SQL commands would be treated as invalid. The database was secure.

Colleagues at other schools told me that we could expect users to write inefficient programs resulting in full table scans and other sinful practices. I feared that if allowed full reign to write and run their own programs, they would seriously compromise system response time for our many online users. We considered prohibiting them from running SQL programs during prime time, but that would probably discourage them and reduce their effectiveness, once again. We finally decided to work with them and hope for the best. It turned out to be a good decision. There were a few problems, but the users were sensitive to system performance issues. If they wrote a program that ran too long, they usually aborted it and called Computing Services for help.

Computing Services was prepared to offer assistance to the new power users for some time. As it turned out, some staff time was required at first, but soon a collection of programs were created that required change only when something new was needed. The users rarely wrote a new program from scratch and they seldom called on us for help after a couple of months.

BENEFITS

Since the end users could now get information from the database, they felt empowered. There was a clear political benefit. When they called or met with Computing Services staff, they no longer felt that we had the power and the knowledge and they had to ask for our help to get what they needed. Their information could now be obtained directly from the computer. The two groups were on more equal footing and the working relationship improved.

There was less work for Computing Services programmers now that some of it had been turned over to its clients. The reduction in the workload was not huge, but it was noticeable. In effect, the programming staff had been enlarged—the development team now included SQL programmers from outside the Computing Services department. The programming solutions were sometimes better. If not better, they were certainly faster. The users learned the structure of their data very well. Also, they didn't need to articulate their desires to programmers who sometimes didn't understand the use of the data. It was much easier and quicker to eliminate the middle step and just tell the computer what was needed.

Some of the new power users became more interested in their work. By adding an activity to their workload that was challenging and fun, they found their whole job more rewarding. They discovered what many programmers already knew. Programming is fun. Developing programming solutions compensated for their routine tasks.

The users now felt that the computer people had few secrets from them. They had become a member of the fraternity because they knew the secret handshake called SQL. A trust developed between Computing Services and Business Services that had not existed before the training. They became more open and honest with each other and worked as members of the same team with a larger common goal.

CONCLUSION

The solution that Southern Oregon State College found to satisfy users' needs for more information will not work in all cases. It worked well at SOSC for several reasons. The size of the school was a benefit. It is small enough that the number of users that had to be trained and supported was few; however, training those few satisfied most of the critical needs.

Another reason for success is that Computing Services carefully selected the class participants. They had to be able to learn the concepts quickly and also have the time to do the work. Since the users enjoyed their new programming responsibilities, it was easier for most of them to find time to apply their newfound knowledge. Care was taken, though, to avoid choosing people who were already so overworked that they would be even more frustrated by not having the time to program.

Another criteria for selection was a thorough knowledge of the activities in the user department. The participants had to have a broad understanding about their data and about programming needs throughout their particular department. Their level in the organization was not important, as long as they could do the programming.

The approach worked well because the users were told from the beginning that support would be provided after the class. There would not be much time to help them individually, but the offer had to be made. The users were nervous at first, but they were assured that they would not be on their own when they returned to their office. Our hunch worked. Very little support was needed. The users soon became self sufficient and confident of their new abilities. It was important, though, for them to know that they had a security blanket if they needed it.

The computing environment at SOSC is poised to take advantage of further distribution of responsibility and knowledge. As the technology changes, the users will become less dependent on the computing staff. Their support needs will change. More help will be needed with network and access issues. The goal, like that of most colleges, is to provide desktop services that best meet the needs of individual users. In allowing them to have programming access to their data, an important first step was taken. The stage is set for future technical cooperative efforts between computing staff and users.

Chapter Fourteen

THE POLITICAL AND TECHNICAL ASPECTS OF PROVIDING FACULTY ACCESS TO ADMINISTRATIVE DATA

Albert C. Leiper
Director of Computer Services
University of New Haven

BACKGROUND

As Director of Computer Services at the University of New Haven, a medium-sized, but fairly comprehensive institution of higher education located in south-central Connecticut, I oversee a staff of twelve professionals charged with supporting both academic and administrative users. Academically, the University consists of five schools and thirty-five academic departments. Administratively, there are three divisions: Day, Evening and Graduate. Physically, the main campus comprises 73 acres and 22 buildings, including a new Admissions Building completed in the summer of 1992. The University also maintains a satellite campus in southeastern Connecticut.

In the past four years, we have completely overhauled our administrative computing facilities and our campus network. In the process, my department has evolved from a centralized, nearly autonomous entity, to a service department for a fairly distributed computing environment. We did this without any changes in personnel, which created substantial problems in and of itself. As computing professionals, we have had to overhaul our technical skills as well as our philosophical approaches to computing.

In the past year, the University itself has undertaken sweeping organizational changes: a reorganized and streamlined Board of Trustees, a new President, a new Provost, a new Vice President for Institutional Advancement, and the adoption of an institutional Strategic Plan. The Plan, adopted in June of 1992, calls for increased faculty involvement in University governance and computer literacy on the part of all faculty.

135

Prior to the Strategic Plan, computing policy and direction were determined by two committees: the MIS Committee, formed in 1988 to oversee the acquisition and implementation of a new administrative computer system, and the Academic Computer User's Committee (ACUC), formed in the autumn of 1991 as a joint faculty/administrative committee to "improve the effectiveness of academic computing and information management."

The Strategic Plan calls for combining these two committees into a single unit, the University Computer Committee, chaired by the Director of Computer Services. The ACUC and the MIS committees will become subcommittees for academic and administrative users. The chairs of these committees form an executive committee to report recommendations to the University officers, who will make decisions on university computing. The Plan also calls for the implementation of a "Students First Policy" and the adherence to the principles of Total Quality Management.

It is against this backdrop that the initiative for what became known as the Faculty Access Project began. The next few pages attempts to describe, in general terms, some of the technical, as well as some of the not so technical, aspects that drove this project. The latter might well be termed "political" because, in any highly complex organization where decisions are made concerning scarce resources, a certain amount of competitive posturing is inevitable. Conversely, as politics is the "science of compromise," we always managed to "work things out."

DESCRIPTION OF FACILITIES

Our current administrative computer system consists of a Digital Equipment VAX 6220 running VMS and the POISE system from Campus America. Our campus-wide network was installed by Southern New England Telephone Company (SNET) and is based on Ungermann-Bass intelligent hub technology. We also maintain Novell and Pathworks LANs, a Data General MV/15000 minicomputer, and a sizable population of microcomputers and UNIX workstations.

The POISE system includes modules for registration, admissions, student billing, fiscal reporting, alumni/development, payroll, and degree audit. Financial aid is supported by the MICRO-FAIDS system from the College Scholarship Service. Campus America provides an interface module between MICRO-FAIDS and the student billing module. The primary tool for developing new applications on the administrative computer is DMS-Plus, the file management system provided by the POISE system. Under DMS-Plus, the basic developmental units are the record description, the menu, the screen, the form and the batch control file (BCF). Record descriptions provide the means of defining data elements and their relationship to each other. Menus provide an easily maintainable user interface to screens and batch control files. Screens provide for interactive file maintenance and inquiry. Forms provide for creating mailing labels and personalized letters. Batch control files provide for general file maintenance and report generation. Most of the POISE modules are built upon DMS-Plus and are, therefore, highly customizable. Within a batch control file, the following processes are possible: file creation, selection, sorting, report generation (including pre-printed forms), updating, labels, and form letters.

Using DMS, a generic menu system was established for all administrative accounts. This system consists of a main administrative menu, which is common across all departments, and two main submenus. The two submenus consist of a POISE menu that allows access to the standard POISE system, and a UNH menu that allows access to local enhancements to the POISE system.

PROJECT SUMMARY

Faculty access to administrative data is not a new concept at UNH. Prior to the POISE conversion, the student records database consisted of many disjoint files, one for each division and term. For users who wanted "read only" access to this information, a system was set up to copy/convert the "live" files, on a daily basis, to corresponding flat files so that reports could be generated using a generally available report writer. In most cases, users created their own reports independent of the Computer Center.

With the conversion to the POISE system, this capability was lost, at least temporarily. Integrated as it was, creating daily copies of the database was prohibitive. Providing unrestricted access to the live data posed too great a security risk.

While the issue of read-only access to student records system had surfaced many times during the implementation of the POISE system, it was pursued with little fervor because we were not sure how to grant such access to the then existent Registration module. The POISE routines (which provided for class rosters, student schedules, and transcripts), were tightly coupled with the routines used to modify the database. These routines were written in VAX Basic. The menus themselves were part of the Basic programs. To remove the items that write to the database would have required modification to the source code, a practice we have avoided except in rare instances.

What appeared to be a major technical breakthrough occurred in the latter part of 1991, when Campus America announced the introduction of a "software switch" that, if set at login time, would limit many of the functions within the registration system to read-only access. As it turned out, this switch was not sufficient to our purpose since its effect was not consistent across all functionality. It did, however, provide some of the spark to pursue the matter further.

Another factor that influenced the start of the project was the formation of the Academic Computer Users Committee (ACUC). This committee, composed of representatives from the schools of the university and several members from Computer Services, made the project a high priority goal for the 1992-93 academic year. This focus led to a series of meetings in January, 1992 that defined the scope of the project and allocated the necessary funding.

The initial objective, termed Phase I, was to provide access to deans and department chairs, a total of approximately 35 offices spread over five buildings. To this end, thirty thousand dollars was committed to provide for the necessary equipment, including wiring. The level of funding was based upon the assumption that approximately two-thirds of the offices had most of the required equipment. The preliminary target date for completion was set for April 1, 1992.

The relatively short time span for the project was based primarily on the condition that, at least initially, we would offer the same functionality as we were currently providing the Library (a system that allows checking student authenticity at the circulation desk). That is, no commitment to additional software development was made.

When we initiated the project, we assumed most of the faculty offices were wired for data communications. As it turned out, none of the offices had been wired (SNET had turned its attention to the new Admissions Building), and by the time they were (around the first of May), we had time to do a significant amount of software development. As a result of the delay caused by the wiring, the target date for completion was changed to August.

The Faculty Access system was initially developed with the expressed intent of providing faculty access to Student Records for the purpose of student advisement. Phase I placed facilities in the offices of deans and department chairs. The base workstation configuration consists of an IBM compatible microcomputer running Procomm Plus emulation software, an attached printer (parallel port), and a direct connect (serial port) to the campus backbone.

Distinct VAX accounts were assigned to all deans and chairs with the understanding that these accounts would be shared with other faculty within the respective schools and departments. These accounts are both "captive" and "read-only": the former meaning that users cannot break out of menus and procedures by pressing a priority interrupt; and the latter meaning changes to data files are prohibited.

Account functionality includes the ability to display/print transcripts, class rolls, and student schedules, as well as a number of reports showing open, closed and canceled courses, current enrollments, faculty assignments, and faculty loading. Access to budget information is provided to deans and department chairs. Accounts also provide access to VMSmail and the 20/20 spreadsheet. Faculty may also upload and download files and display the status of batch and print queues.

The project required wiring for thirty-five offices and the purchase of twelve new computer systems with printers. Software purchases included thirty-five copies of Procomm Plus, a terminal emulation program in wide use on campus (as an expediency, we purchased copies for every prospective user in lieu of determining which existing copies were "legal"). A user manual was developed (currently in its third revision) and ongoing training and support provided. Planned enhancements include access to the Degree Audit system and the establishment of an electronic bulletin board.

PREPARING THE USERS

Initial contact with the users was through questionnaires, which attempted to ascertain what equipment was already available and to have users begin thinking about where and how to deploy the equipment. While we did suggest the consideration of space requirements, furniture, and availability of electrical outlets, in retrospect we should have been more direct and more detailed. We should also have stressed the logistics and problems of having a departmental microcomputer within a dean's or chair's office.

Even the best of questionnaires will not overcome the need for a structured walk-through. Users may not know such things as whether they have a data jack available or what kind of connector is required to connect to their serial port. In addition, some faculty may have been on sabbatical when the project was initiated.

DOCUMENTATION AND TRAINING

The preparation of user documentation began concurrently with system development, as did preparation for training. In fact, we regarded the two as almost inseparable: to attempt to conduct training sessions without written procedures or to provide documentation without accompanying human contact would have been equally futile.

To provide for the training, we wired one of the student laboratories and installed Procomm on the PCs. In this endeavor, we made every effort to avoid any disruption of student use and scheduled around classes.

We conducted several training sessions prior to actual installation, but despite our preparations, realized only about 50 percent attendance. We have found that the most efficient approach is individualized training at the user site. This is easier to schedule, can be tailored to individual needs, and has the added benefit of discovering and correcting idiosyncrasies in the individual configuration.

Documentation for a group as diverse as this one, in terms of both people and equipment, presents a significant problem. In the case of the former, it is best not to assume too much (our procedures manual is a veritable picture book) and, in the case of the latter, it is best to assume almost anything (I know of at least one PC on campus that was built from a kit). Even in the most standards conscious environment, it is inevitable that individuals will customize DOS environments (or install Windows).

To contend with the diversity of equipment, we made two assumptions: that Procomm was installed in a subdirectory, called PCPLUS; and, consistent with Procomm's documentation, that all users would be starting from the DOS prompt. We also found that the distribution of the documentation can present some problems. Providing an up-to-date document of about fifty pages to as many as thirty to forty faculty members is quite time consuming. As it is the intent of the project eventually to provide access to all of the approximately 165 faculty members, we are considering alternatives to a printed manual. One approach would be to place the documentation on the VAX computer and make it accessible via a menu item so that any user wanting an up-to-the-minute copy could print his/her own.

TRACKING USAGE

Tracking of faculty usage began in August of 1992. This was facilitated in part by public domain software obtained from the DECUS Library. At this writing we have four complete months of data.

Basically, we capture five items: number of logins, access time, processor time, number of images executed, and number of pages printed. The last of these (pages printed) applies only to queued print devices and, consequently, has no significance at this time. The first four may give some insight into usage, but we have, as yet, made no attempt at interpreting the data, partly because of the short period of observation (we expect the data would have minimal seasonal fluctuations).

Although space constraints and confidentiality issues do not permit revealing the specifics of this data, I have taken the liberty of preparing a graphic representation depicting the general usage traits (Figure 14.1). To do this, I arbitrarily invented a statistic that combines the four samples into a single measure. This statistic is calculated by normalizing the scores in each sample, applying a weight of ten to each score and taking the sum. A perfect score would result in a value of forty. Figure 14.1 does not show that very little user migration took place from month to month between scoring groups. In other words, a user with a score of twenty in August will have a score of approximately twenty in September.

SECURITY

The VMS operating system provides two methods of file security—the long-standing User Identification Code (UIC) and its associated protection mask, and the newer Access Control List (ACL) and associated Rights database. Under the UIC method, each user is assigned a unique number pair: the first number denotes membership within a computing group, the second is usually unique to each user. Access rights to a given file are then determined by its ownership stamp (specified by UIC) and its associated protection mask. The protection mask categorizes all users relative to four security levels: system, owner, group, and world. For example, the Registrar might have a UIC of [401,1]. The STUDENT file would be stamped with his UIC and might have a protection mask that allowed read and write access to anyone in the 401 group.

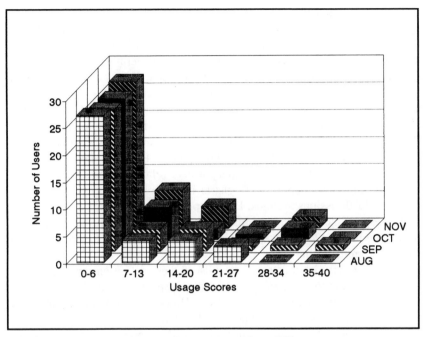

Figure 14.1 Monthly Usage: August-November 1992

This scheme works well for the half-dozen people in the Registrar's office. They can have their own individual accounts (with unique UICs) and yet have read-write access to Student Records by virtue of being in the 401 group. But what of other workgroups who need only read access? Obviously, they can not be given "system" status or placed in the 401 group. The only alternative is to set the protection mask to allow read access to the "world" (everybody on the system).

At UNH, we recognized this deficiency in UIC protection as soon as the VAX system was installed and, consequently, have depended primarily on ACLs for database security.

Without knowing the genealogy of the POISE system, I would hazard a guess that it evolved in much the same way that many home-grown systems do; that is, by addressing the specific operational requirements of an administrative office, vis-à-vis the Registrar. Other enhancements and other modules were added in time to make the product marketable.

POISE training and installation guidance reflected this orientation. Workshop attenders generally consisted of staff from an operational department plus computer personnel and advice on computer security centered around the UIC code. Thus, in terms of the type of access we were seeking, we were pretty much on our own.

Early in the implementation of the POISE system, we adopted a terminology and a philosophy to help us deal with the question of informational access in a quasi-integrated environment (the POISE system is integrated only if all users are granted equal access rights to all data). One term we defined was that of "Prime User" (this could cause some confusion if you happen to have a Prime computer on your premises). The Prime User for each POISE module was defined to be that person responsible for the integrity of the associated database. So, for example, the Registrar is the Prime User for the Student Records system, the Dean of Admissions for the Admissions system, and the Controller for the Fiscal Reporting and the Student Billing systems.

All others were dubbed "secondary users" relative to one or more systems. Within this scheme, the Registrar is a secondary user relative to the Fiscal and Admissions systems. Based upon these precepts, a Prime User is solely responsible for access to his or her respective module, and Computer Services will not add, change, or delete user accounts without written authorization from the Prime User.

Computer Services unilaterally established these definitions and policies as a means of arbitrating access requests and/or disputes. So far, they have gone unchallenged. Considering that most Prime Users come from middle management, however, we foresee some potentially interesting scenarios.

Accompanying these definitions, we created a hierarchy of access classes within the file security system of the VAX computer. For example, the STUDENT master file might have an access control list that defined a Class A user as having read and write access and a Class B user as having only read access. Similarly, the access control list associated with the General Ledger file might define a Class C user as having read and write access and a Class D user as one with read-only access. The Rights database would then list the Registrar as being both a Class A and a Class D user. A faculty member could be listed as a Class B and a Class D user.

METHODS OF PRINTING

One of the most difficult issues to resolve involved the method of printing/displaying reports and various other forms such as schedules and rosters. It is relatively easy to display them on the screen (although some problems with using monitor displays are discussed later) and several of the printing methods are contingent upon this capability. A number of methods were considered to provide printed reports produced on the VAX computer:

Screen Printing

Displayed output is accomplished by simultaneously pressing the <Shift> and <Print Scrn> keys while the desired output appears on the screen. This works reasonably well for output that fits conveniently within the 80-column by 25-row display, but is unsatisfactory for wide reports that span several pages.

Another downside to this method is that the PC indiscriminately prints everything on the screen, including Procomm's "Help" banner.

Log Files

The Procomm software allows a screen capture mode to be toggled on and off during the terminal session. The captured text is stored in a "log" file on the user's PC as an ASCII text file that may be printed at any time. It can also be edited prior to printing to remove undesirable text.

Downloading

Using the Kermit file transfer protocol, it is possible to download the complete text of a VAX print file (including carriage control characters) to the PC, where it may be printed using the DOS PRINT command.

Queued Print Devices

The output is sent to a printer connected directly to the network. Each such printer requires the establishment of a separate print queue on the VAX. Although faculty members preferred this method initially, it is laden with problems:

1. Most buildings have several floors with faculty offices on each floor, a faculty member advising a student on the third floor might have to retrieve pertinent output from a printer on the first floor.
2. Who would or should retrieve the output? The faculty member may not want to leave his office unattended. The student may not know the location of the printer or how to operate it.
3. Suppose no one retrieves it? Confidential information would be left in an open and easily accessible area.
4. Space at the university is at a premium. The prospect of finding an unoccupied room to house a printer would be unrealistic. The prospect of finding an occupied room with an occupant disposed to accepting the attendant traffic and noise would be equally unrealistic.

We briefly considered having the output queued to a Computer Center printer. This would have ensured confidentiality, but would have defeated the purpose of having the data quickly available when advising students. While the faculty has not abandoned the idea of queued printers altogether, there is currently no pressure to pursue this option, due largely to the general acceptance of the Print Controller mode of printing.

Print Controller Mode

The POISE system is designed around the functionality of the VT320 terminal. When displaying transcripts, for example, the VAX software remotely sets the terminal to 132-character width.

The VT320 terminal also has a printer port which allows the connection of a "slave" printer. By placing the terminal in a "Print Controller" mode, terminal output from the VAX passes through to the printer. What is more, this mode can be set remotely by sending an "escape sequence" from the VAX computer to the terminal.

Originally, we had proposed this "plug-and-run" solution for all faculty not having equipment. While this approach provided a simple and inexpensive solution to the printing problem, it was not acceptable to ACUC representatives because of the limited functionality of a "dumb" terminal: that decision changed the scope of the project, i.e., we were no longer simply attempting to provide faculty access for student advisement but, rather, in a subtle way, providing for other microcomputer-based features.

We actually developed some prototype software with this approach in mind—an effort that, as it turned out, was by no means wasted. We discovered through what might be termed a "happy accident" that the Procomm software supports the Print Controller Mode.

This breakthrough was perhaps the most significant in the entire project. It meant that any faculty member with a networked microcomputer, an attached parallel printer, and a copy of the Procomm software could receive quality hardcopy output right at his/her desktop.

SCREEN DISPLAYS

A requirement of the Faculty Access project was to provide as an option the capability to display all printed output to the terminal screen. This feature is built into the POISE system provided a VT-style terminal is used. POISE simply changes the terminal width remotely and "TYPEs" the output. Using a Hold Screen key, the user can pause the vertical scrolling at any time for closer examination of the data. A downside to this approach is that upward scrolling is impossible (to view a portion of the report which has scrolled by, it is necessary to restart the procedure).

While PC monitors that support 132-column displays are available, we were obliged to use mostly existing equipment that do not. Consequently, we were forced to deal with displaying 132 columns on an 80-column screen.

Fortunately, Procomm has Key Commands for paging left and right, which solved the screen width problem. Nonetheless, users still expressed displeasure over the inability to scroll upward. We addressed this with a quick-fix by using the VAX EDT editor rather than the TYPE command for displaying reports. The combination of EDT and Procomm gives the user the ability to page up, down, left, and right. For a more permanent solution, we are investigating the EVE editor, which permits split screens, and its underlying product, TPU.

CONCLUSION

These few pages described some highlights of our attempt at UNH to provide access to administrative data for members of the academic community.

While we finished on schedule to original specification, the Faculty Access Project at UNH is far from complete.

Already we are receiving requests for more enhancements. In fact, "Faculty Access" is becoming something of a misnomer. Other offices are expressing an interest in gaining similar access to the database. And lest we forget, the left-most bar in the chart from Figure 14.1 indicates that more work is probably required in the areas of computer literacy and user friendliness.

Through the project, I have come to know a much larger segment of the University community and have developed a number of valued contacts at other institutions. In particular, I would like to thank Mr. Edward Donahue and Mr. John Vasily from Babson College for sharing their ideas and financial software with us. I would also like to thank UNH professors Dr. Brad Garber and Dr. Baldev Sachdeva for serving as our "beta sites."

And lest someone draw the impression that I might be POISE-bashing, I want to point out that that software brought us out of the computer "Dark Ages," and it was through their annual User Group meeting that we met our contacts at Babson. Lastly, while I alone take credit (and responsibility) for preparing this case history, the Computer Services staff performed the lion's share of the work.

Chapter Fifteen

DISTRIBUTING ADMINISTRATIVE COMPUTING INFORMATION TO THE CAMPUS

Arthur Brooks
Director of Administrative Data Processing
University of Missouri-Rolla

BACKGROUND

Located near Interstate Highway 44, midway between St. Louis and Springfield, UMR is one of four campuses of the University of Missouri. Founded in 1870 as the University of Missouri School of Mines and Metallurgy, this campus enrolls approximately 5,000 students, consisting primarily of engineering and science majors.

Administrative Computing

Since 1975, nearly all of the University of Missouri system's administrative computing has been handled at the Central Computing Facility (CCF) in Columbia, ninety miles to the north. These core systems are resident on an IBM 4381 and an IBM 3090 class computer using CICS as their online data manager. Most of the systems utilize VSAM files with the student system using IMS and the Alumni system currently changing from IDMS to DB2. In order to fund the central facility, campuses are charged for all computer usage on a consumption basis. Since this facility operates on a zero-based balance, the computer rate structure is very flexible.

The support staff at the Central Computing Facility provides all direct core system programming support. The staff handles any computing activity required to maintain the core systems. Campus represented user groups define and recommend all systems modification requirements to the CCF programmers. With this concept, the campus computing staff operates in an ancillary mode—any campus computing needs that cannot be satisfied by the CCF personnel fall within the relevant domain of the campus staff.

Campus Computing

All campus computing is under the direction of the Director of Computing Services, who is responsible for the Campus Computing Center and Administrative Data Processing. The Campus Computing Center staff of twelve programmers has among its responsibilities the maintenance of the mainframe operating systems, support of the campus LAN servers, and technical assistance primarily for faculty and students. Several years ago the campus administration opted to totally fund Computing Services from general operating funds, eliminating the long-standing practice of charging users for local computing services.

UMR currently has two IBM 4381-class computers running the VM operating system. Within the last three years the campus computing staff has installed a campus optic fiber backbone for networking the seventeen LAN servers and various UNIX servers. Connectivity is provided using ethernet via eight unshielded twisted pair telephone wires. Essentially all campus servers use either the Novell or Apple-talk platform. Currently, the campus's upper management offers strong encouragement to attach *all* faculty and appropriate support staff to one of the campus LAN servers. It appears by July 1993 that that objective will be very nearly accomplished [see Addendum to this chapter for current status], increasing the number of devices attached in this manner to well over thirteen hundred.

Administrative Data Processing

The department consists of a director, a secretary, four programmers and one production controller. This office has the responsibility for providing technical support to administrative users on the UMR campus as well as handling programming requirements for a multitude of campus specific reports, which are too numerous to be addressed by the CCF staff. Technical support is provided to the entire campus when difficulties with corporate systems connectivity arise. With the introduction of PCs to the campus, PC technical support, training and advice to administrative users has been added to the expectations of the user community for this office. Due to the meager size of the staff, daily activities can range from writing programs, to advising on PC configurations, to installing personal computers. In addition, ADP manages the campus's budget for administrative computing at the Central Computing Facility and manages a campus computer time purchase fund.

One programmer and the production controller are dedicated exclusively to the support of applications software production, primarily the student system. Traditionally, what little development activity that could be afforded was handled by the three other programmers and, when possible, the director contributed to the effort. Unfortunately, modifying existing programs, writing new reports from the existing systems, and fighting technical "fires" left little time to consider development of any new applications in that environment. Development was more of an apparition than a tangible entity.

THE PROBLEM

From the middle of the seventies through the middle of the eighties, computing activities and expenditures steadily soared as more and more administrative systems were added and expanded. Every year the financial requirements at the central facility increased as did the needs for campus technical support. Concerned with the accelerating demands, the Director of the Office of Administrative Data Processing annually stated the office could not begin to keep strides with the growing requirements for computing support from the campus administrative users—but those requests have never reached high enough in administrative priorities to be fulfilled.

Campus administrators initially were willing to support financially the demands of the burgeoning core systems. With passage of time, limited budgets, and change of administrations, however, demands were placed on the Office of Administrative Data Processing to curb the rise in spending. ADP had to find ways to meet the campus administrative computing needs without increasing costs. Every option to reduce computing activity was tried, making sure there were no adverse affects on the operation of the custodial offices. Unfortunately, the efforts were successful only in reducing the acceleration of spending, not curbing it. Over a period of sixteen years, the administrative computing expenditures have been at or under budget only twice.

All administrative systems reports were written in Mark IV and run at the Central Computing Facility. To keep costs down and to avoid conflicts with daytime activities, all reports had to be run at night or on weekends. Consequently, program development was measured in days, as any keying error or logic error cost the developer a full day in development. While the selection of Mark IV as a reporting method was a significant productivity tool compared to Cobol or PL/I, development of any new report remained an arduous task.

By the mid-eighties, the number of Mark IV programs written by the ADP staff for the student system alone numbered over five hundred. To aid in the creation of parameter cards for each run and to reduce the technical requirements for program submittal, a series of CLISTS were written. While these routines helped reduce the demands on the programming staff, software maintenance still exacted significant energy. In addition, the client base for program requests was expanding to the point where, due to insufficient staffing, an increasing number of requests were denied, or given a pocket veto.

SEEING THE LIGHT

Knowing something had to be done to address the onslaught of demands on administrative computing and to keep spending in check, the Director of ADP began in 1985 to search for other solutions. The focus was strictly on alternatives that could improve programmer productivity while maintaining the level of service demanded by the custodial offices and on ones that showed the potential to reduce costs. Since all computing activity at the CCF was billable, no consideration was given to that facility as a logical location for whatever solution would be proposed.

Because the local computing facility, which was providing computing services for academic uses only, did not charge for computing, the potential for using the campus's IBM 4300 computers was the first step in the search. It was determined that sufficient computing power was available to handle the projected administrative requirements, providing an IBM 3380 was added to handle the anticipated increase in DASD storage.

Having identified a cost-effective computing solution, the most important requisite was now programmer productivity. After investigating possible alternatives, it was decided Structured Query Language (SQL) seemed to hold the most promise. This software was on the list of IBM consortium software that could be made available without cost to the campus—too good a deal to pass up.

In the spring of 1986, two ADP programmers were assigned the tasks of learning more about SQL (as their workload permitted), and determining whether it was feasible to operate the platform in the UMR computing environment. They were charged with assessing the difficulty in downloading the core system information to the local facility, in converting the existing data to the new platform, and in estimating the ease in writing reports. Their basic responsibility was to determine whether SQL offered a viable solution to a serious problem and whether the ADP staff could accomplish its successful implementation.

THE PLAN

Having concluded the database platform was viable and achievable, the campus data custodians were called together in September of 1986 and informed of the plans for implementing this new technology. The reactions to the announcement from the data custodians ranged from apathy to less than enthusiastic. None of them could appreciate the problem nor the growing dilemma. Their basic approach focused on their own needs for funds because of their departments' perceived strategic importance to campus operations.

Since the student system was the largest of all of the campus systems, with the highest costs and the greatest demand, it was decided to extract a logical portion of that system to the campus facility and load it into three SQL tables. The original focus for data extraction was on the primary report requests; i.e., address and biographical data on prospective and currently enrolled students. Also included was enough course enrollment information to provide faculty with the ability to download class lists at the beginning of the semester. This proved to be the first SQL application placed into production on this campus. Since the Registrar believed the data was not that dynamic, it was decided to download the information three or four times each semester. Additionally, the decision was made to create an SQL table strategy which corrected the perceived faults in the student system's basic design structure and eliminated many of the inane system codes for ones better understood by the programmer assigned to develop and support the local SQL tables.

THE FIRST LESSONS

In less than a year it was learned data had to be downloaded more frequently than a few times each semester. This became quite clear as the programming staff began to replace Mark IV programs, which cost the campus money, with SQL queries (reports) that had no financial charge. Additionally, it was learned the first cut on the downloaded data definition was extremely deficient. As a result, after conferring with the Registrar, the frequency of data downloads was increased to once a month, and the SQL download definition was expanded in a second iteration.

From this meager beginning, the programming staff of ADP learned SQL indeed held great promise for the campus. It was clear this platform could replace *all* of the hundreds of Mark IV programs, which were expensive to run. Moreover, a single programmer could produce countless queries in a single day, whereas one Mark IV program had always taken several days to develop. It was also confirmed that downloading data to the local mainframe computers would save the campus money while expanding ADP's capabilities. This was an impressive solution for addressing the burgeoning requests for services while keeping expenses in check.

An important realization from this beginning was the determination that an individual did not have to be a computer professional to create an SQL query. This method of reporting was so straightforward that many of the campus users could be trained to write their own reports. Such a solution held promise in addressing the dilemma of the suffocating number of demands for extraneous reports. It also offered the potential to allow the campus an avenue by which to enter the realm of the electronic informational system, a developing environment and an attractive administrative perspective.

In the final phase of development of this iteration, the ADP programming staff determined that a set of rules had to be drawn before full production of local downloaded SQL tables could be initiated. The rules developed were as follows:

1. Only needed data would be downloaded, not entire systems.
2. The campus download efforts were to provide enhancements or extensions to core systems and would not attempt to duplicate existing services from the Central Computing Facility.
3. Access authorization to the SQL tables, download specifications and data interpretation were to be kept in the domain of the data custodian for that data.
4. Any activity associated with the SQL platform was the exclusive responsibility of the Office of Administrative Data Processing.

5. Levels of access had to be succinctly defined.
6. A schedule of downloads would be established, adhered to, and made known to the data custodians.
7. Downloaded SQL tables would be autoloaded, eliminating the need for a programmer to work late nights and keeping maintenance out of the productive office hours.

In addressing the question of access, three levels were clearly definable. The first level, requiring an absolute minimum amount of training, would allow an individual to have only query access to SQL data. A second level of access, with additional training, would allow an individual to have query access and to submit stored SQL queries. With still further training, the third level would allow individuals to write and store their own queries. This latter select group could fundamentally be viewed as an extension of the ADP programming staff. In effect, it would represent the increase in staff that had been so badly needed, but never seemed to arrive.

STRUGGLING

During the first two years of downloading with SQL locally, progress was relatively limited. The staff had much to learn regarding SQL's characteristics, table idiosyncrasies, terminology, and system strategies. Continuing demands for services in other areas constantly took the staff away from the download activity. Also, in mid-1987 and then again in mid-1988, the programmer assigned the responsibility for the SQL effort left the university. In one year two different programmers were assigned to the project and both resigned to accept jobs in other states. The staff had another individual who was talented in an extensive variety of computing activities and had some knowledge of SQL, but his talents were desperately needed to keep the other activities viable. Without the proper expertise and staff commitment, the SQL effort would die.

Fortunately, in the fall of 1988, we hired an individual who had the professional skills and the interest to take the campus fully into the distributed computing environment. Since he had no knowledge of campus systems, the decision was made to direct all of his efforts to the SQL project. While from the beginning this venture has been a team effort involving the entire ADP programming staff, that one staff member has been the key to the success of the relational technology on the UMR campus. In a very short period of time he learned SQL, installed SAS/SQL, and wrote a local SQL system for maintaining the campus equipment inventory. In addition, in response to a request by the Personnel Office, he began designing the SQL tables for downloading portions of the university's Payroll/Personnel systems. This was the needed spark to have this critical endeavor succeed.

Within six months the staff determined SAS/SQL was entirely too slow, bringing about the decision to cancel the license at the end of the first year.

After a brief review of available software, the staff selected QMF as the tool with which the campus users would write reports from SQL tables. This decision required a rewrite of the equipment inventory system, but a change that, in development terms, required minimal effort.

IN FULL STRIDE AND A NEW BEGINNING

Early in 1989 the Registrar was taught to write his own queries against the locally resident SQL student system tables. That May, the ADP office in conjunction with the Personnel Office conducted SQL training for one staff member in each of the three academic dean offices and the Office of the Vice Chancellor for Academic Affairs. These individuals were trained in basic SQL concepts, QMF techniques, and data characteristics to allow them to write their own queries against the Payroll/Personnel system.

Quite soon the Registrar realized the second iteration of data definition for the student system was grossly inadequate. Far too many data items were missing, the information was not current enough, and the local data construction confused him. He had also discovered he needed access to historic information to satisfy the requirements for a growing number of requests for campus reports. Consequently, the download schedule was increased to once a week, and a complete redesign of the student system tables was initiated.

One of the beautiful aspects of the relational model of processing is its capability to handle major table (file) definition modifications without affecting the data. Making system changes in the IMS environment is a major undertaking; requiring data unloads, system redefinitions, and data reloads. In SQL, changes in one table can be made without affecting either the data in the table involved or any of the other logically associated tables. Major table redefinitions are basically inconsequential to the applications using them.

In the third iteration of the student system, it was decided the best table design was one which emulated the IMS file structure of the student system at the Central Computing Facility. That data scheme was one already familiar to the Registrar and would eliminate occurrences of report irregularities that the second table definition inserted. Surprisingly, it was found very easy to replicate an IMS structure in a table oriented scheme. That hierarchical system could in fact be replicated precisely in the relational mode. In the redesign each SQL table was defined to closely imitate an IMS segment in the core system.

The data download definition was increased to the extent that nearly all of the student data was now to be downloaded to the UMR campus mainframe. The number of tables increased from the original three in the first iteration to thirty-one in this design (not counting "frozen" files and other tables created for auxiliary reporting). These newly defined tables included not only student address/biographical data, but student transcript, current student course enrollments, current course offerings, and catalog descriptions. In addition, all codes were returned to the student system's original values. The information downloaded now contained all students enrolled since 1980 as well as current and prospective students. With concurrence from the Registrar, the ADP staff decided to download all dynamic student data after midnight every Monday morning. More static data, such as catalog and course information, would be downloaded at intervals relevant to the data characteristics or upon demand of the Registrar.

After we had completed the expanded definition of the local student data, the Registrar became very active in writing his own reports. Instead of referring requests for reports to the Office of Administrative Data Processing, he proudly began handling many of these requests himself. At his request the ADP staff created a table of the dates of the downloading to allow him to determine the currency of his data in the various tables.

For the first time the Rolla campus was now able to address requests for reports which combined information from both the student and the personnel systems. Such requests were so difficult in Mark IV that the few futile efforts never succeeded. Now with SQL, combining disjoint tables was as simple as naming the tables and data fields needed. A significant void had been filled by a technique which would be used commonly to report jointly from many of the campus's locally resident administrative systems.

During 1989 the Office of Institutional Studies expressed a need to do extensive reporting from the student system and from the personnel system. A new computer literate staff member was added to that office and, with the permission of the proper data custodians, OIS was given access to financial aid, payroll/personnel and student systems. Because of the department's need for static data, the procedure of making census data tables ("frozen" reporting files) locally available was implemented in order for it to produce additional and more definitive reports, using the same data from which published statistics had been produced. With this capability the Office of Institutional Studies has been very active in generating its own statistical reports for the Office of the Chancellor.

To allow the Office of Administrative Data Processing to make progress with the SQL efforts, a closure was placed on all Mark IV efforts at the Central Computing Facilities. The statement was made that (with few exceptions) any Mark IV program that needed to be run, modified, or written would be generated in QMF against the local SQL tables. This statement was not welcomed by the Registrar, but the move had to be made. Despite intermittent complaints from the Registrar, the decision was adhered to and new reports were created without affecting the schedule of the requesting users. Rather than embarking on rewriting *all* Mark IV programs in a single massive effort, new QMF queries were written against local SQL tables as requests for the Mark IV programs were received. Consequently, the conversion took well over a year, but did not have a noticeable impact on the workload in ADP, nor did it adversely affect the campus user community.

CONFIRMATION OF THE ENDEAVOR

After six years with the relational environment, the Rolla campus of the University of Missouri now weekly downloads portions of the student system, the cashier's system, the financial aid system, the payroll/personnel system, the loan system, and the accounting system. Currently, the grant system and the campus-written budget system are being reviewed for a rewrite on the local system as well. Also, new applications have been written for equipment inventory, student admissions (prospective students and applicant tracking), and a departmental/student telephone tracking and billing system.

After this length of time:

1. Only a scant handful of campus-written Mark IV programs are still in production.
2. The costs for reports to end users have been reduced by eliminating the computing charge from the Central Computing Facility.
3. A campus user can now have a requested report complete in only an hour or two rather than several days. (Such spontaneous requests are not encouraged, but it is a significant boon to be able to do so under unusual circumstances.)
4. Programmer productivity has improved impressively.
5. Requests for reports from disjoint systems are now being processed.
6. User access to corporate data for reporting purposes is now possible without jeopardizing the core systems and without interfering with production activity, because all local activity is restricted to locally maintained tables and not at the site of the live data.
7. Campus expenditures at the Central Computing Facility have been reduced with further reductions projected.
8. Computing activity greatly increased without the addition of a computing professional.
9. The Office of Administrative Data Processing has advanced from being an office totally dedicated to writing miscellaneous reports and maintaining JCL to one that actively develops new applications for the campus.

To date:

1. Of the corporate systems (accounting, alumni, financial aid, grants, library, loans, payroll/personnel and student) only alumni and library do not have data downloaded to the campus or consider the move at this time.
2. Seventeen users in twelve campus departments have been trained to write SQL queries. (These departments include offices such as the Dean's offices, the Computer Science department, Student Loan Office, and Human Resource Services.)
3. Campus userid authorization, profile, and maintenance utilize SQL and have access to student and payroll/personnel data.

4. Since 1987, members of the faculty have been able to download an electronic class roll to a CMS account or to a PC to create their grade book for the semester. This routine accesses the current student course enrollment table.

5. In 1991 an electronic bulletin board was made available to the campus community (students and employees) to provide them an electronic view of a variety of campus public information. From the Registrar's portion of this electronic information system, an individual can review the course catalog since 1980 and the current schedule of classes. (Both of these items are downloaded from corporate systems.)

6. Also in 1991 electronic telephone directories were provided to the campus. From two separate directories a user can retrieve the current local address/telephone for the student requested or the current office address/telephone for the selected employee.

The identifiable costs to the Rolla campus over the six years:

1. $7,500 for a used IBM 3380 storage device.
2. $7,500 for one-half share of a used IBM 4380.
3. Approximately $800 per year for weekly downloading data.
4. $1,500 for SAS/SQL for one year.

CULMINATION OF PHASE ONE

As this document was being written, a routine was going into production to provide students with the ability to query their own fee status from the Cashier's Office, telephone billing information, address data, and biographic information. Discussions have been held with the Registrar to expand this to include GPA, current class schedule information, and transcript data. With further development it could be feasible to provide such additional services to students as address correction online, transcript requests, and student surveys. Next in the queue is an online employee address query and update capability. When complete, this will be the first campus application to upload data on a continuous basis to a core system from a local SQL application.

After trying to deal with the myriad requests for reports, a state reached by ADP years ago, the Registrar decided in October of 1992 that he cannot keep pace with the demands for reports he has received from the broad spectrum of campus users. Consequently, he has taken the position that selected users should be able to execute stored QMF queries at their discretion rather than burdening the Registrar with their frequent requests. To initiate this venture, he has asked the Office of Administrative Data Processing to provide each of the three academic dean's offices and the Office of Academic Assessment the ability to access a defined set of stored queries. The bulk of the queries available to them will be queries the Registrar has written. As new queries are created, he will add the appropriate queries to those available to the users. The indication at this time is that such services will be expanded to other campus offices when the technique has been adequately refined. This has been a significant decision in the evolution of distributed processing at UMR. A decision which was preceded by several years of "debates" between the Registrar and the Director of Administrative Data Processing.

Throughout the length of the project the question of data download frequency has continually arisen. It is the conviction of the ADP staff that a weekly download schedule will not be sufficient much longer. As more and more campus users are provided the ability to access the local data, the need for more frequent downloads will become necessary. Users will simply not tolerate waiting until the next Monday to run their reports. Whether the next change in frequency will be to every night, Sunday through Thursday, or something less than that is still to be decided. As has been the case throughout, the reduction of CCF expenditures to offset the increased cost will be a detemining factor.

There is no doubt the venture into the realm of distributed computing has been an overwhelming success for the Rolla campus of the University of Missouri. Nonetheless, the time to draw closure on this phase of the conversion to relational processing has arrived. Due to their age and technology, the local IBM 3380 and 3370 storage devices have failed frequently over the last year. Similarly, the IBM 4381 processor is outdated and is now viewed as less than reliable for production activities. To date these devices have served the campus well. They have adequately handled the admissions system, the largest of the campus SQL systems, which has over one hundred and fifty users, while continuing to provide computing power for all SQL applications and other non-student activities. Unfortunately, the tools to provide a more user-friendly SQL relationship is not realistic with the current mainframe environment. GDDM has been the software with which all users access the locally resident data. The time to initiate that software for each user or to bring up QMF in the VM environment has normally taken forty-five seconds. That length of time is intolerable and elicits the most frequent complaint from users. Consequently, in this phase UMR has progressed as far as hardware and software will allow.

THE FUTURE

In 1991, ADP staff members realized that a new computing environment had to be found if the campus was to stay with the distributed concept and if further progress were to be gleaned. After extensive discussions with campus systems staff, it was decided ADP would chart a course of action to take local administrative computing activities from the IBM 4381/VM environment to RISC/6000 processors using AIX or UNIX. With that in mind, Oracle and Informix were evaluated in the spring of 1992 and an IBM RISC/6000-220 has been acquired for development. With a new version of Informix released after the spring evaluation, Informix has been acquired for a second review, and we submitted a bid to procure a software package that provides the range of database capabilities suitable for the needs of the campus.

Considerations are currently being given to the logical definition of the hardware on which to house the new database platform. The advantages and disadvantages of a single, large RISC system verses several smaller RISC systems have been discussed for some period of time. A statement of initial direction to some processor strategy will be made fairly soon. When the equipment and the software are in place, the ADP staff will be in a position to open discussions on venturing into the client/server realm; a reality provided by the success with SQL.

In July 1992 the Chancellor of the Rolla campus announced an intent to eliminate all paper processing on the campus. The first step in that process (Personnel Action Forms and absence reporting) was completed by July 1993. At the heart of this commitment is the new UNIX relational platform. This statement of direction from the administration clearly presents a very large challenge for a staff of few people. While the associated tasks will tax the abilities of the staff, due to the advantages of the relational realm, those tasks are viewed as possible to achieve in a phased approach. Six years ago, the staff would have simply melted away at the prospects of attempting such an incredible assignment. The future couldn't look brighter.

WHAT HAS BEEN LEARNED

1. The relational technology is vastly superior to more traditional methods. From all perspectives it is a very exciting environment.
2. The complex level of security in SQL and its design flexibility are extremely impressive.
3. A single SQL table or set of tables can be defined by the DBA to present different images to different users depending on the requirements of the user.
4. Users can be trained to write reports from administrative systems, striking down the antiquated position that database access should be reserved for a select few.
5. The most critical ingredient in the success of user written queries is the training in data characteristics. The matter of SQL concepts is secondary.
6. Computing directors must have patience in dealing with data custodians. They have legitimate reasons for conservatism and an acquired fear of new techniques that can threaten the stability of their operations. This does not mean capitulations on the part of the computing director, but a combination of encouragement and understanding. Assurances have little affect on users when their existence is involved. A director of com-

puting must continue to explore and promote new computing techniques, but realize that advancements are not going to come quickly. This is especially true if staff size is insufficient to carry the improvements to quick fruition. Change comes slowly.

7. Data custodians can be expected to vacillate with time, especially if the idea was not their own.

8. To the users the relevance of the future is perceived through the perspective of the current time and current problems.

9. Progress does not come with a continuous advancement, but rather ebbs and flows.

10. Creativity must be accompanied by optimism, enthusiasm, and a great deal of planning.

11. User expectations can frequently be anticipated as unrealistic and short-sighted.

12. The user community must make the mental adjustment and acceptance of the new methodology before the technology can be successful.

13. Computing directors must remember where there is a will there *really is* a way.

CONCLUSION

In reviewing six years of work, one must ask the question: was it worth it? In our case, the answer is a resounding yes! The journey into the realm of the relational systems has been a most satisfying one. While the basic concept is simple, the power it possesses is incredible. It truly does bring the corporate data resources to the hands of the end users, providing them with the ability to use that information as their position requires.

No longer is it a requirement for the computer professional to be the mystic medium between the user community and the computer-stored data. Instead, the efforts of those highly trained individuals can be concentrated on more technical activities and they can rely on the relational platform to provide a significant productivity tool when needed.

Of all of the data custodians involved in this effort over the last six years, only one has been in opposition at any time. The Registrar has vacillated between being mildly helpful and being totally resistant. He is also the only participant who did not approach the Office of Administrative Data Processing with a request for local computer activity. Since he did not request the service, he did not see the need for variance from the core system at the Central Computing Facility. In addition, my twelve years of experience in the Registrar's Office and participation in the design of the current student system provided me with exceptional insight into the operation of that office, but also provided a threat in the mind of the Registrar.

Depending on the day and the topic, he has made positive comments regarding this project and severely criticized it in the same breath.

If I have erred in handling this project it is in approaching the Registrar with new ideas at a rate faster than he was willing to consider. Time and again I have made suggestions for new consideration only to receive a firm, if not irate rebuff. Consistently, however, the Registrar has presented those same ideas to me one to two years later. With the seemingly abrupt request from him to provide departments with the ability to submit their own queries, ADP has at last seen the implementation of a campus informational system that was foreseen four years ago. The transition to the new perspective in administrative computing has been slow, but it has evolved with time.

How gratifying it would be to state this development in administrative computing at the Rolla campus was the result of a masterful plan conceived seven years ago. This case study clearly reveals that was not what transpired. There was no well-orchestrated revolution, but rather an evolution that began from desperate needs to improve productivity and reduce costs. The success has resulted from keeping our minds open, a talented staff, and a magnificent computing platform. This chapter presents proof that an enormous staff of programmers dedicated to the project is not required to distribute corporate information to the campus community. With the client/server strategy on the horizon, ADP is standing at a new threshold. Clearly, UMR has a firm foundation for administrative computing in the nineties and has developed the ability to chart the course that will maintain an optimum position in the distributed environment.

It would have been preferred to have concluded this document with a succinct statement of a savings of "X" thousands of dollars as a result of our venture into distributed computing. Unfortunately, that is not possible. Over the last several years, the Central Computing Facility has continually lowered its rates. Concurrently, there occurred an unending number of enhancements to the core systems, countering the cost reductions and the savings from our downloading activities. What can be stated with certainty is that the Rolla campus has new applications and a multitude of reports being prepared that could never have been afforded with the budget constraints in both computing and salary/wage accounts. That is a significant statement without even viewing the enhancements in performance and access to corporate data.

In my view, having implemented the foundations of a campus informational system with only one full-time programmer assigned to the project and with extremely limited financial resources, proves the power of the environment. Under such circumstances the progress must be measured in millimeters, but it does exist and the director must be convinced of it. Having seen first-hand the fruits of our labor, I believe it is imperative for an organization to cast aside the traditional perspective in data processing and make the transition to informational systems. It does work and it is worth every bit of the effort given.

ADDENDUM: 1994

The original portion of this document was completed in December of 1992. In the time which has transpired since then, the following is a summary of what has occurred:

1. In April, 1993 the campus was required to submit a compliance statement to the Environmental Protection Agency. As a result of that;
   a. The Office of Administrative Data Processing was asked to develop an automated chemical tracking system and an electronic MSDS (Material Safety Data Sheet).
   b. In September, 1993 an HP 9000/755 was purchased to support the chemical tracking system and for local administrative computing.
   c. In October, 1993 Informix software was acquired as a platform for all campus local database activity.
2. In October, 1993 the campus employees were provided with the ability to view address/spouse/salutation type data and update the information online.
3. In October, 1993 an employee social register table was created for the Chancellor.
4. In February, 1994 the local student information procedure (STUINFO) was amended and readied for production to allow students to update addresses online.
5. In March, 1994 a survey option was added to STUINFO.
6. With the acquisition of the HP hardware and Informix software, the UMR campus was ready to consider downsizing and client/server options. In conjunction with that;
   a. Planning has begun to remove the VM-based IBM 4381 mainframe computers and re-tool with UNIX on mid-range computers.
   b. Work has begun to identify a tool for campus users to access the campus data warehouse.
   c. A procedure was developed to load Windows from a LAN and to restrict usage to authorized users only.
   d. The concept was implemented to identify a "Windows coordinator" in each administrative office.
   e. Campus wide Windows training has been initiated to establish the base for the anticipated client/server activity and to eliminate 3270 communications protocol.
7. In March, 1994 effort was initiated to convert the student information procedure (STUINFO) to UNIX using Mosaic and WWW.
8. Forty-one people can now write/submit SQL queries.
9. Enough cost savings was seen in expenses to the Central Computing Facility in fiscal year 1992-93 to allow the campus to re-wire the telephones in several of the buildings on campus in preparation for LAN access and to partially pay for the HP platform.

10. The fiscal year 1993-94 has seen the introduction of telephone registration which has increased computing costs to the campus, but the anticipated expenditure is still significantly lower than fiscal year 1991-92. The cost advantage hoped for in the beginning of this project has perhaps been finally realized.

PART THREE

Using Older Systems

CHAPTER SIXTEEN

WORKING WITH AN OLDER DATABASE SYSTEM

Thomas A. Warger
Director of Computing Services
Bryn Mawr College

INTRODUCTION

The professional literature offers many articles and much advice on adopting new technologies. The time lag between emergence and acceptance for new tools and techniques is shrinking. Yet there is little written for those who, for whatever reason, continue with the old. The purpose of this chapter is to survey the issues of working with an older database system. It does not argue against change, but neither does it hold that older systems are static and incapable of being changed or used more effectively. In perhaps no other aspect of information technology is the replacement of the old by the new as difficult as in the succession of central database systems. The cost is dismayingly high, and the diversion of time and attention from primary duties further taxes an institution's administrative staff.

Most computing centers in higher education are probably facing the need to continue using older systems. An informal survey of representatives of the Consortium of Liberal Arts Colleges meeting at the 1992 EDUCOM national conference showed that more than 75 percent were examining newer alternatives to their current administrative computing software. By the same token, those institutions probably consider themselves to be working now with an older database system. Many have only known one generation of comprehensive database computerization and have no experience with complete replacement.

The reasons for staying with an older system vary. Some owners think their database system has still a lot of life in it. It is trustworthy, well-understood, and (highly important in times of austerity) paid for. Some would change but can't afford to do so—for a university it costs millions and for even a small college at least half a million dollars. Some institutions see no appeal in the prospect of major expenditures for new technology. If the payroll runs, stu-

165

dents are registered, and administrators at all levels get their monthly reports, what is broken and in need of fixing? Some are preoccupied with other priorities. Declining enrollments, rising insurance costs, escalating demands of regulatory agencies, and the expansion of student services are all examples of costs that compete with expenditures for information technology—even as they lead administrators to draw greater benefits from their database systems to meet these problems. Some do not yet see an alternative sufficiently advanced over the capabilities they now have to warrant the expense and upheaval of changing. Still others are biding their time, hoping that a conversion to a new system will somehow become affordable and easy. After all, those who stuck with their Cobol code long enough lived to see automated means for rewriting and translating it.

WHAT QUALIFIES AS OLD?

The definition is easier in the negative. The older system is not "open" or "standards based." It may have been created in the era when everyone thought computers would never exchange information, or that auditors would tolerate it. Or the standards might have been particular to a vendor or even a single programmer/analyst, and not "standard" at all in the current sense of the term. The older system is not based on one of the currently dominant general purpose database packages. Software in this category has either been original to what we now call industry standards or has generally kept pace with those standards. For the most part, software that has not been particularly successful in the commercial market has not generated the funding to support keeping up with changes in technology.

The older system is likely to be "proprietary" (vendor-captive) or of a technology with no obvious prospects for evolution. Pick-based systems would be an example of this latter type, though many Pick loyalists would dispute that view. Some older databases have found new vitality by being overlaid on newer technology, such as the downsized RISC/UNIX environments that have largely supplanted minicomputers. But even this example shows the difficulty of definition, as UNIX by itself is anything but new and at least as old as some of the database technologies in question. Others of the older systems have been so highly modified and customized over time as to bear little resemblance to the original, or to anything else. Administrative database systems tend to accrete new code in response to local needs and often without an explicit strategy for long-term maintainability and eventual portability when the basic system is replaced.

STRATEGIES FOR WORKING WITH THE OLDER SYSTEM

Writing in *CAUSE/Effect* magazine, Gene T. Sherron [Sherron, 1992] lists six options as the domain of choices for those with aging systems. They range from immediate replacement, through methods of gradual or partial replacement, to staying indefinitely with the existing systems. When asked to rank these in order of preference, respondents from CAUSE-member schools generally preferred to begin a full or gradual conversion to new software, but one third replied that they would keep their current systems for a while and half foresaw a hybridized system of flat-file and relational databases.

Three basic strategies exist for working with the older system: continue as before, complement it through other technologies and methods, or begin building bridges to what will eventually replace it. Properly speaking, strategies imply explicit commitment to a planned course of action. They also proceed from a focus on major institutional goals and observe particular constraints. All too often purported strategies lack one of these qualifications and, instead, represent rationalization for a course of action whose origins are unclear (except to be called "historical") and whose intended outcome fails any test for specificity.

Strategy #1: Stay The Course

The first of the options for working with the older database typically does not come about in a way that would truly qualify it as strategy. Rather, it is a set of arguments for not raising the issue of change to a strategic level. But strong cases can be made for the significant value of postponing the replacement of the older database system, and they deserve to be evaluated as a potential strategy.

Established systems often have unappreciated value in their continuity. The three watchwords for administrative computing have been "stability," "reliability," and "security" [Cossey and Ringle, 1992]. In the well-maintained older system, defects and unpleasant surprises have been driven down to near zero. The high costs in time and talent absorbed in the early phase of its life cycle are in the past and are now superseded by a favorable ratio of benefit to cost and, presumably, a progressively lower cost of ownership over time. If the institution has been amortizing or otherwise preparing for the system's eventual replacement, postponement of the changeover date has a direct financial benefit. If no preparation is made, then the postponement is more accurately the product of neglect than strategy.

Educational institutions are usually averse to risk and, ironically, reluctant to change. Postponing the upheaval and expense of a major change in databases feels right in the absence of crisis or imminent problems. Delay takes on more substantive justification when other claims exist on funding and projects priority. Allowing that a strategy of holding the old can be established, several tactical consequences follow.

As long as the horizon does not clearly indicate that the database system can no longer continue on its course, it should be exploited to its fullest capacity. Program additions and modifications whose costs are justified can create greater value. Extension of access to more users who would benefit from it also builds value at relatively low cost. A thorough review of usage will likely show that some of its capabilities are being neglected by client offices that don't know about them, that generally underuse the system, or that have not yet developed their practices to levels of functionality designed into the system. A combination of continued applications development and renewed efforts to educate its users would offer increased value from the older system.

A moratorium on new development in the old system would be a basic principle once a determination has been made that its future is approaching a limit. Almost certainly, that rule will result in a constant rearguard battle, and a path littered with exceptions. Administrative practices are not static, and so the new demands on the database system will never cease—but the absence of curbs on new development, once the end of the system is acknowledged, would only compound the difficulty of the eventual transition. In practice, a halt in new development runs a serious risk of conflict between the database managers and their clients if it is not coupled to a schedule for a new system or some alternatives that will deliver the desired advances. Functions judged to be seriously deficient in the database might be turned over to service bureaus ("outsourced") or moved to specialized standalone systems as interim measures. Calling an end to customization will certainly not sit well with clients who see the prospect of indefinite stagnation.

There is, however, another line of reasoning for a moratorium. Older systems tend to drift into a condition of "reactive maintenance" [Woody, 1991] in which programmers only intervene to fix problems. These patches accumulate and, eventually, the maintainability of the database system becomes increasingly tenuous. What was once reasonably clean and efficient is now encumbered with fixes, changes, and additions that have not followed a consistent plan but, instead, have been improvised to meet the pressures of the moment. In this perspective, every further change ultimately threatens the stability of the whole. In fact, this tendency is an argument for planned obsolescence. One of the uncomfortable truths in database programming is that while most of the work is of the remedial kind, the best talent and most attention are drawn to development projects. Thus, database systems have tended to deteriorate in quality over time despite the best intentions of those who manage them.

Given adequate resolve, and the appropriate staffing and management, it should be possible to re-visit the code of an older system in the aim of lessening the effects of prolonged maintenance programming. Variances in coding style due to changes in practices over time or to the influence of staff with different approaches might be reduced by rewriting patched and appended code sections to a more rigorous standard. Redundancy and bulk in the code would be other targets for improvement: they typically reflect work done in a hurry and might be consolidated in new code produced under more disciplined circumstances. The result should be cleaner code that runs more efficiently and is easier and cheaper to maintain.

If the older system can retain a favorable balance of cost and benefit it should meet the needs of a strategy based on cost avoidance. If that system can bear continued development to add functionality at an acceptable price, then it might have a strong claim to viability. But time acts against these considerations. Technology has enhanced system productivity constantly, though the trend has not been sufficiently powerful to guarantee similar improvements for personal productivity. In this light, continued investment in an older system could be considered a poor practice once the opportunity costs of replacement become favorable. It is not necessarily the case that cost avoidance is best served by continuing with the existing database system.

Strategy #2: Shift Focus

The second strategy for working with the older database is to shift focus to the wider context in which information processing takes place. (The central database system is, after all, only part of the more extended picture of information management.) This strategy has the goal of progress in the exploitation of information as a resource when changing the database itself is, for whatever reason, not elected. There is less urgency to replace the center, as the real opportunity for improvement in information systems is seen to lie elsewhere.

The focus has been stated this way: "Don't be seduced by technology. The soul of a true management information system is not the machine—it is process, culture and information. Do it right and you may not need expensive technology at all" [Alter, 1992]. The computer is one of a set of interlocking parts, others of which are people and their activities. This strategy recognizes that technology is not the sole determinant in the success of an information system. Advances in effectiveness can be made without changing technology if other aspects of the larger process can be improved. In this view, the database system might actually be the element least amenable to improvement and, therefore, least important to change. The major opportunities lie not in the machine.

For most of the age of computers, the pride of place has been claimed by the central data processing shop, whose authority rested on its supervision of transaction processing. This organization was synonymous with information management; but as decentralization and dispersal of computing have become the main tendencies, the role of the central database and its human handlers has changed [Clark, 1992]. Systems design and development have become less important than systems integration. The developers have become advisers. Nobody is expecting the largest gains in productivity to come from a better database engine or improved query tools, though these might figure in an overall reworking of the process.

If programming staff can be redirected and retrained to help their client offices reach a better understanding of how work flow and information management can make better use of the database system as it exists, then gains in usefulness can still be squeezed from the older system. Probably every campus records database package has menu items, screens, and reports that have been neglected by client offices or forgotten since the original installation. In some instances they may contain useful features perhaps not appreciated earlier in the office's experience with automation. Computing Center staff could be used to help those users explore previously unused capabilities that are within reach. To be sure, this tactic requires a change of thinking on the part of computing professionals. But when an older system is kept, and development ceases or reduces substantially, the time and talents of the programmers are available for new duties, if the hearts and minds are willing.

Another direction possible under the strategy of shifting focus is to concentrate on software tools outside the database system. In the past decade, office automation computing has thrived without any particular relation to the purposes and procedures of the database environment. Only recently have microcomputers installed for this function been equipped as terminals to the database host. Word processing alone accounts for a very large share of the productivity gains realized through computers in office settings, with spreadsheets not far behind. To some extent, these developments have distracted managers from improving the central database. Downloading to spreadsheets, desktop databases, or merge-mail routines join the capabilities of the newest microcomputer software with data extracted from the central system. If data fields can be selected for extraction to a file that can then be transmitted to a microcomputer, the older database system need not be the host for new reports, correspondence, or spin-off applications. The key to methods involving downloading is to insure that the original database remains the authoritative repository of information. One-way transfers of information, repeated as necessary to refresh the downstream application, enforce the dominance of the source database. While uploading data to create a two-way flow of information is desirable, many older database systems were not designed to accommodate automatic imports of data and are incapable of checking for data integrity without substantial program modifications.

Standalone applications, particularly specialized ones run typically on microcomputers, are an alternative to adding new functionality to older databases. Databases for dining services, physical plant work orders, campus parking permits, hazardous materials inventories, and other locally administered services need not be written as extensions to the main transactional database. Here, too, downloads of data to these systems are valuable and uploads, though desirable, are not indispensable.

New procedural and technological adjuncts to the older database offer ways to extend the usefulness of the system without need to modify it or to write these functions in the outmoded technology. At the same time, they shift attention from the limits of the old to the possibilities of supplementing it with newer methods and tools. As administrative staff members master their microcomputers, their expectations in software performance rise. If they are not enabled (and encouraged) to link their new skills with the information in the older system, their impatience with the differences will only increase and lead to frustration with the system they would prefer to change but cannot.

Strategy #3: Build Ahead

The goal under the third strategy is to prepare for change while observing the constraint that a smooth transition is required. There can be no gap in time or loss of information between the cessation of the old system and the start-up of the new. Consequently, the old and new will need to coexist for an interim before the replacement can be declared ready. But even before the commitment is made to change systems, steps can be taken to anticipate how the old prepares the way for the new.

When the older system must remain in an environment where productivity gains are demanded yet awareness of the limitations of technology constrain project ambitions, a method of bridging from the old to the new is good. New and old systems can be linked through "interim code" [O'Leary, 1992] that enables an existing database system to work in tandem with applications built on technology platforms that promote access across system boundaries. The interim code consists of instructions enabling the reach back from the new to the old, and might eventually even become expendable when the older database is finally replaced. The presumption in these circumstances is usually that the older system undergoes no significant modification.

The database that must be carried forward (sometimes termed the "legacy system") can be enhanced by several noninvasive methods. The simplest of these is to upgrade the hardware that runs it. Where system response time can be dramatically improved, the payback can be seen in productivity and staff morale. If the new hardware platform includes higher communications speeds that support faster transfer of electronic files, a trend to more processing of downloaded data might be the result, again without alteration to the principal database. "Wrapping" an older system in new software that provides a windowed interface and streamlined means of data extraction is still another way to bring some of the appealing features of current technology to the old via retrofitting.

The most ambitious approach to revitalizing an older database system is to "wrap" it in new technology. Software that provides a windowed interface, report generator, and streamlined downloading/uploading can make the system appear new and, in important ways, perform like new. Some alteration to the older system might be necessary to fit the new wrapping, but the effort will be considerably less than a conversion to new, basic software that would produce the same functionality and appearance. Placing an extra layer of software between the user and the computer extracts an inevitable cost in performance, but one that can be met through hardware upgrades. A version of this method is used by some major administrative database vendors who emulate client/server technology by putting a Z39.50-compliant query routine between the user and the (older) database's native query engine.

The recognition that gains in productivity through greater automation accompanied by work force reductions are mostly in the past fuels the interest in "reengineering" [Penrod and Dolence, 1992]. If incremental thinking dominated in the past, when bigger-faster-better was manifest destiny, then systems upgrades and replacements were the order of the day. But with current thinking more inclined to look for advances through changes in process, stepping up to the newest level in technology is no longer an obvious benefit.

The term "reengineering" in information technology represents awareness that simply replacing old hardware and software with new is not a sufficient approach to improvement. Instead fresh analyses of the relationship of work goals and processes to the technical means for carrying them out are undertaken. Projects of this kind are notable for the scope of participation they require within the work force. By the same token, the changes they bring affect more than just the computer-based work and workers.

To be sure, most discussions of reengineering call for adoption of new tools for new methods. But the practical demands of implementation argue for prolongation of the older system, while the new is laboriously developed and proven. The construction of a new information management system at the Georgia Institute of Technology [Martinson, 1992] is just such a case in point. Their "technology transition strategy" seems likely to require a decade to accomplish in its full extension to all administrative offices. Most of the time the project is devoted to the mobilization of people and the coordination of their methods and work flow. Specifying the elements of the database system in the context of that exhaustive analysis must precede each phase of software development.

While administrative units await completion of their modules of the new system, their older database systems are still in effect. Furthermore, the old serves as a benchmark for the new: the replacement must at least match its predecessor on every aspect of functionality or be judged a failure. The cost and disruption occasioned by the process of changing systems leave users with little tolerance for loss of any previous features, and the successor system actually needs to perform substantially better to be considered worth the pain.

HIDDEN RISKS OF THE OLDER DATABASE SYSTEM

In several respects the older system poses risks that derive not from intrinsic flaws but from the circumstances in which it now operates. None of these is easily remedied or compensated. These risks also share the characteristic of becoming progressively stronger over time. All are most amenable to being contained by having a strategy for working with the older system, so that the reasons for bearing their cost is known.

1. *An outdated view of information management.* Systems that are now ten or more years old were typically designed for operational support of administrative work and to be used by clerical staff. The goal had been to gain productivity in routine tasks through automation. At best, a few management reports were included for control and review of those activities, but supervisors and office heads were not foreseen as users and the system was not designed to accommodate their work. Executive summaries, longitudinal data history, and ad hoc query capability—all now standard features of database systems—are usually not found in the older systems. The danger is that their lack perpetuates the idea that information management is just "data processing," a clerical task. Because not all managers feel at ease with information technology, some will feel reinforced in that view by the limited perspective of their institution's database system.

2. *Future staffing difficulties.* When the state of information technology in a workplace falls behind the standard of the day, the institution risks problems in retaining staff who are aware of that discrepancy. And, when it loses a key programmer for a system that is no longer widely used outside the organization, replacement may be difficult. Outside the computing department, difficulties in staff recruiting at all levels might ensue if top prospects for open positions decide that the institution's information management system appears antiquated and not up to the standards of their experience.

3. *Lack of preparedness to change.* Occasionally, the impetus to upgrade systems comes from outside. At a college or university, the influence might originate with an outside evaluating committee, the auditing firm, or the board of trustees. Though the campus administration is comfortable with its current systems and methods, these might be judged inadequate by an off-campus constituency. If the result is need for sudden change, the transition could be formidable.

4. *Inability to work in the "open" environment.* Campus information systems are evolving to standards that promote a degree of access and interoperability that older database systems never foresaw. Database hosts on campus local area networks are inherently less secure than in times when they did not share wires with students and faculty, much less the rest of the world via Internet. The system that requires an uncommon screen emulation or that cannot communicate over TCP/IP cannot be integrated to a wider network without unusual and onerous special arrangements. In some instances, faculty at last obtaining access to registrar records for their advisees have found the (older) administrative database's access and menu methods awkward. At one time the technical isolation of administrative and academic systems was thought a benefit. But those same barriers are counterproductive in the now-standard campus networks.

5. *Impatience.* Administrators and their staffs are becoming better informed about the state of practices in computing. Their colleagues, professional publications, and the general awareness of computer trends lead them to assess their institutions systems in a more demanding light. They might find them deficient on practical measures but also on grounds of image or prestige. The older system can thus exact a toll in morale resulting from general impressions that users have about its obsolescence.

CONCLUSION

Colleges and universities (and some administrative database vendors, for that matter) have various reasons for needing to continue working with systems that have been superseded in the technical arena. Often, the very success of the database systems they have developed contributes importantly to the difficulty of change. The high degree to which the organization of work depends on computers has left no tolerance for time without them. There is no opportunity to uproot the old and replace it with the new. Cost exerts an increasingly steep barrier to systems replacement. While hardware has gotten steadily cheaper, software has not, particularly where systems need to be customized from a base model or to be written directly from specifications. For all these reasons strategies to extend the usefulness of database systems that cannot evolve gracefully should be developed. Failure to take a comprehensive and forward looking course of action now can lead to chaos when the older database system is no longer workable.

REFERENCES

Alter, Allan E. 1992. Silicon Valley Civics. *CIO*, 5:17.

Clark, Jr., Thomas D. 1992. Corporate Systems Management: An Overview and Research Perspective. *Communications of the ACM*, 35:2.

Cossey, David and Ringle, Martin. 1992. The Role of Administrative Computing at Liberal Arts Colleges, in *Computing Strategies in Liberal Arts Colleges*, edited by Martin Ringle: Addison-Wesley.

Martinson, Linda. 1992. *New Directions in Financial Computing: Integrated Administrative Data Processing in Higher Education*: NACUBO.

O'Leary, Meghan. 1992. How to be Wary Without Waffling. *CIO*, 5:8.

Penrod, James I. and Dolence, Michael G. 1992. *Reengineering: A Process of Transforming Higher Education*. CAUSE Professional Paper Series, #9.

Sherron Gene T. 1992. Old Systems Never Die . . . They Just Age Us. *CAUSE/Effect*, 15:1.

Woody, Carol. 1991. Evolution of an Aging Information System at Yale. *CAUSE/Effect*, 14:4.

PART FOUR

Long-Range Plans

CHAPTER SEVENTEEN

REENGINEERING CAMPUS ADMINISTRATIVE INFORMATION SYSTEMS

Glen W. Turney
Director of Administrative Computing
Kenyon College

"Reengineering" has recently become a common term in discussing the status and direction of campus administrative information systems. Most current administrative application software is designed around hardware and software capabilities ten to fifteen years of age. Since then, advances in computer hardware and communications networks have far outpaced advances in administrative software. Applications developers are therefore in a position of playing "catchup" to build administrative computing systems, using the latest technical tools, that better serve the campus community.

At first glance, reengineering administrative systems seems to be a large task with high risks. Every administrator remembers a past computer system conversion and shudders at the thought of again facing that experience. But past problems can be avoided with proper communications, planning, organization, and use of new computing tools. An old saying advises that you "eat an elephant a bite at a time." The secret is to make the project "bites" as small as possible and "eat" them in the right sequence.

The discussion of the reengineering process must start with a review of administrative computing objectives and an understanding of the current status of applications systems. A review of new technology follows to provide the basis for the establishment of a new systems approach. Next, the issues of systems implementation must also be understood and, last but not least, the reengineering of administrative systems must provide a benefit to the campus community.

ADMINISTRATIVE COMPUTING OBJECTIVES

The historical objective of administrative systems can be stated as follows:

Improve the administrative efficiency of the departments of the enterprise.

This objective has been oriented to administrative departments for two reasons. First, successful computer systems are built to support and improve the operation of a specific function or organization. Since departments are the primary organization unit of the campus, current systems were built to support specific departments. The second reason is that old technology did not effectively support anything beyond a departmental unit.

But the reengineering of administrative systems should center around a much broader campus-wide information objective, expressed as:

Improve the administrative efficiency of the total enterprise.

Improving the flow and processing of information between departments, as well as within departments, will bring efficiency gains for the total enterprise. Current network technologies make this approach reasonable and viable.

Campus Wide Information Systems (CWIS) are currently appearing on many college campuses. A CWIS stores and displays information. It consists of news, bulletin boards, information announcements about campus activities, and other topics of general interest.

Using current network and database management technology, a campus-wide administrative information system (CWAIS) can be implemented in an enterprise to better support administrative functions.

CURRENT SYSTEMS

But before discussing the CWAIS approach, we should review and understand the current status of administrative systems. As previously stated, information files and systems do support, and thus mirror, the campus structure and functions. Since the campus is organized and structured by departments, current administrative systems are department oriented. A brief review of current systems illustrates the need to consider reengineering.

The current departmental administrative systems are shown in Table 17.1.

When systems are department oriented, information must flow between departments via the paper network, which consists of stacks of documents and/or reports. The documents are processed and/or generated in one department, received in another department, batched, and entered into the department system. Next, a series of batch runs are processed to update files and print reports.

It is interesting to note that the reports generated by each department system add to document flow within and between departments. A report from one department system may become input to another department system.

The existing systems, used for department processing, are not easy to change. They were either bought by departments from outside developers or

Table 17.1 Departmental Administrative Systems at Kenyon College	
DEPARTMENT	SYSTEM
Admissions	- Admissions - Financial Aid
Registrar	- Registration - Student Records - Degree Audit
Student Affairs	- Student Housing - Student Advising
College Relations	- Alumni Development
Finance & Administration	- Accounts Receivable/Student Billing - Personnel/Payroll - Purchasing/Payables - Fixed Assets - Fiscal reporting (General Ledger, Budgeting, and Reporting)
Maintenance	- Shop Order - Inventory

built by a central group of on-campus specialists. The systems therefore must be revised by the vendor or the local computing specialist staff.

Also, the development tools used to build current administrative systems had limited functionality. When improvements in database management systems (DBMS) and applications development tools occur, they are slow to be utilized in all systems because of the time requirements of upgrading and conversion.

Most vendors of administrative software offer a DBMS that is proprietary to that developer's specific applications. This means that the vendor built the DBMS and is thus required to upgrade and maintain the DBMS in addition to the applications. Therefore, additions and upgrades to the proprietary DBMS functionality are limited. A number of conclusions can be drawn from a review of current administrative computing application systems:

1. Clerical time is required in each department to create, receive, and maintain the paper network that feeds departmental systems.
2. Access to current information is difficult because it consists of data residing on the system plus the stacks of documents in transit.
3. Revisions from a vendor or central applications group are time consuming, creating an applications backlog and a continuing wider gap between systems' requirements and systems' performance.

4. Therefore, "shadow" systems and files appear on less expensive department PCs to satisfy information requirements not met by the departmental system.
5. This, in turn, creates duplicate information files in different departments on different hardware/software platforms.
6. Additional systems are required to maintain duplicate files.
7. Thus, additional management and clerical time is required to maintain duplicate files and systems.
8. Finally, the creation of duplicate files and systems also creates errors and file discrepancies that must be continually resolved.

Reengineering current administrative systems into a CWAIS environment provides the opportunity to improve administrative efficiency of the campus by reducing paper flow, duplicate systems, and duplicate files.

THE CAMPUS-WIDE ADMINISTRATIVE INFORMATION SYSTEMS APPROACH

The CWAIS approach is different from current systems approaches. The CWAIS focuses applications development on campus-wide functions as opposed to individual department functions. In the process, departmental information needs are satisfied, in addition to the achievement of campus-wide efficiencies.

The first step in implementing a CWAIS is to identify file categories that mirror and support campus-wide administrative functions, focusing on the customers and resources of the institution. A simple list of file categories that represents, at a very broad level, the administrative functions of the institution is:

> Customers:
> > Prospective Students
> > Students
>
> Resources:
> > Alumni and Friends
> > Employees
> > Facilities
> > Vendors
> > Budget Control (Finance)

The next step is to further define the file categories into subsets. Table 17.2 contains a list of file categories and the corresponding subsets represent the next level of definition. Readers may note that these file subsets may continue to be defined into other file subsets until a manageable level of file definition is reached.

After the file subsets are defined, simple file tables of rows and columns containing fields of information are defined for each file subset. Each data

Table 17.2 CWAIS File Subsets			
FILE CATEGORY	FILE SUBSET	FILE CATEGORY	FILE SUBSET
Prospective Students	Personal	**Alumni and Friends**	Personal
	High School		Family Profile
	Performance		Work Profile
	Activities		Activities
	Interests		Giving History
	Campus Contacts & Visits	**Employees**	Personal
	Application		Campus
	Acceptance		Faculty
	Financial Aid Profile		Payroll
	References		Public Affairs
	Athletic Profile		Salary Administration
			Accounts Receivable
Students	Personal	**Facilities**	Status
	Housing		Capacity
	Advising		Technical Equipment
	Course Scheduling		Communications
	Registration		Asset Value
	Campus Activities		Shop Order
	Performance		Inventory
	Degree Audit		Security
	Health and Counseling	**Vendors**	Vendor Information
	Accounts Receivable		Purchase Requisition
	Financial Aid		Purchase Order
	Student Loans		Accounts Payable
	Public Affairs		Vendor Performance
	Career Counseling	**Budget Control (Finance)**	General Ledger
	Payroll		Budget
	Library		Financial Reporting
	Security		Projects and Grants

field is stored only once in the system. Security levels are defined to specify personnel having update and/or inquiry capability for each data field.

Finally, processing modules are written to update and access specific groups of data fields. Processing procedures can be defined and executed, based on entry of data, thus eliminating the need for much of the scheduled batch processing. This feature is important. It provides the ability to update immediately all defined accumulation fields when the data field is updated. Persons accessing the information online are therefore looking at the latest accumulated information. Processing procedures may also be executed through scheduled batch processing where required.

Data fields may be updated and/or accessed by campus personnel from any terminal on the network according to security definitions. Personnel will update and/or access data fields according to their respective responsibility in the college organization. User friendly interfaces, such as windows, are available to permit users to make choices by pointing and clicking as opposed to entering codes.

It is important to note that the development of a CWAIS is an evolutionary process. Data subsets and corresponding processes may be implemented individually or in small groups, but they must be implemented within the total CWAIS framework.

AN EXAMPLE: EMPLOYEE INFORMATION SYSTEMS AT KENYON COLLEGE

The CWAIS approach has already been successfully implemented on three file subsets of employee information at Kenyon College. The employee information file subsets are personnel, campus, and faculty information. The following outline details the problem, solution, and results of the project.

Employee Information at Kenyon—The Problem:

1. Personnel duties are shared by a number of departments based on the type of employee (faculty, administration, support staff, or maintenance).
2. Personnel information additions and changes were entered on paper forms by different departments and routed through other departments via the paper network to ICS to update the computer employee file.
3. The paper flow system was not reliable, causing the computer file to be incorrect.
4. Because all college departments did not trust the computer employee file, many maintained their own department "shadow" file of college employees based on information received from various sources.
5. Each year it was necessary to send out mailings to all employees to correct the computer employee file, which is a primary input to the campus directory.
6. All faculty information was maintained on paper files in the Provost office.
7. Access to information about particular employees by management personnel was impossible.

Employee Information at Kenyon—The Solution:

1. The overall solution was to have one computer file to represent the official accurate list of campus employee information. This file would be updated and accessed from any department on campus, according to defined security.
2. Computer files were established for personal, work, and faculty information, with corresponding online update screens.

3. Validation files were set up for specific information fields to insure consistency and accuracy of data.

4. A specific group of persons was identified, according to its campus function as opposed to department, as the EMPMAS update team.

5. The EMPMAS update team members were given the ability to update the computer employee information files directly, based on the employee information responsibility assigned to their offices.

6. The EMPMAS team input assignments are:

Office	**Employee Type**
President	Administrative Exempt
Provost	Faculty
Staff Relations	Salaried and Hourly Staff
Maintenance	Maintenance

Office	**Information Type**
Payroll	Address changes
ICS Operations	E-mail Addresses
Registrar	Faculty Voice/Vote
	Procession

Office	**Faculty Information**
Provost	Status, Assignment
	Review Dates
	Committees
Academic Dean	Office Assignment
Public Relations	Degrees, Associations

7. Batch processes were written to examine the file each day for changes and automatically communicate notification of changes to each member of the EMPMAS team via e-mail.

8. Inquiry screens were written to permit general access to the file on selected information.

9. Batch processes were written to daily transfer address information from the employee file to the payroll file.

10. A daily batch was implemented to automatically create e-mail distribution lists for all employees, selected employee groups, divisions and departments.

Employee Information at Kenyon—The Result:

1. Almost all paper flow has been eliminated from this process.

2. The EMPMAS team members have accepted a campus responsibility and have done an excellent job of accurately maintaining their information assignments.

3. Clerical time has been saved in many departments because the improved file accuracy has eliminated the need for individual departments to maintain their own files.
4. Clerical time has been saved in many departments in maintaining departmental e-mail distribution lists.

By using the CWAIS approach, a simple solution was implemented for a complex situation. This simple solution would not have been possible without recent changes in and availability of technology.

This implementation of segments of the employee information system at Kenyon clearly demonstrates that the campus-wide administrative information system approach is workable and improves administrative efficiency.

NEW TECHNOLOGY

A number of technical advances have made the building of a CWAIS possible. These advances include the campus electronic network, improved database management technology and application development tools, faster and less expensive computer processors, and faster and less expensive data storage.

The campus electronic network is one of the most dramatic technical advances: it has literally changed the campus communication culture. The network provides electronic communications between campus personnel as an alternative to the current paper and voice communication links.

Through the campus electronic network, all persons on campus can easily and quickly communicate with each other, as well as with peers from other educational institutions. All administrative personnel on campus can also access administrative computer systems files according to defined security.

The campus electronic network is bridging the current barriers between departments, thus providing the opportunity for the campus to function as one integrated department. This satisfies a basic requirement for a successful CWAIS.

In addition to the electronic network, relational database management system (DBMS) technology is another important technology tool. DBMS packages currently on the market provide a number of important features that are essential to building a CWAIS.

1. Tools to *create and manage relational data tables* provide the ability to store and retrieve data fields in a row and column format.
2. *Data view definitions* of fields from multiple tables provide the ability to access and control data in a logical format that is different from the physical table format. Thus data can be accessed in different logical groupings but physically stored only once.
3. *Security* at the data view level provides the ability to define security for any person to access any logical combination of data fields.

4. A *central dictionary of data fields* is essential for the management of a common DBMS for the college.
5. *Online transaction processing* provides the ability to update immediately the DBMS from any point on the network.
6. *Field level lockout* for online processing insures the integrity of data in an online environment where multiple transactions occur simultaneously.
7. *Online journaling, backup, and recovery* provides data recovery and integrity in case of a hardware or software failure.
8. *Processing procedures initiated by data entry* into a table permits the automatic update of other data fields as a result of online entry, thus eliminating the need for batch processing.
9. *Data inquiry* provides access to all CWAIS data for which a person has security clearance.
10. *Application development tools* consisting of:
    a. *Menu and screen generators* to build online processes;
    b. A *forms generator* to print special forms and custom letters from data files;
    c. A *report writer* to generate and print reports.
11. *Hardware portability* of the DBMS tool to process applications either on the PC, the midrange, or the mainframe processor platforms, provides the opportunity to run the same application system on a desktop or central computer. The flexibility of selecting smaller and less expensive computers offers an additional cost savings opportunity.
12. *Client/server capability* of the DBMS tool is required to support distributed processing. In the distributed processing environment, the database and related processing code resides on a server. Users can access the server via the electronic network, execute computer processes, and access the database using desktop stations as the computing engine. Distributed processing not only provides the opportunity for savings by downsizing to less expensive computers, but also gives improved response time because the desktop devices perform the computing process.

SYSTEM REENGINEERING ISSUES

The first and most important reengineering issue is the support of administrative personnel for the process. It was earlier stated that successful computer systems are built to support the operation of a specific function or organization. Therefore, senior staff backing of the system reengineering project is essential because those individuals represent the entire campus.

In addition, the participation and support of all administrative supervisory and clerical personnel is a must. The environment must be established for all personnel to work together on teams to review current practices and suggest improvements. They must be permitted and willing to think on a campus level, in addition to their department level responsibilities. After all, administrative personnel who do the work on a daily basis are usually the best source of ideas for efficiency improvement.

The second critical issue centers around implementation. The approach should be "evolutionary" as opposed to "revolutionary." There should be no "turnkey" conversions. Such projects cause high stress and are not necessary given the current stability of administrative systems.

The most desirable approach is to shift to the new environment through a series of projects over the next three to five years. Each project should be as small as possible. Highly visible projects should be done first to gain the support and enthusiasm of the administrative staff. Early projects should also be selected that have a high probability of success. Finally, high payoff projects should be done as early as possible.

The "make" or "buy" decision is a third issue. The option of buying the software should be evaluated for each project, but it must be remembered that any system considered for purchase must serve the college information needs. The college should not change its requirements to fit the proposed system. The "buy" decision should also include consideration for outsourcing certain applications.

It is also important to note that buying applications software may not mean buying the latest technology. Applications software vendors are also playing the "catchup" game with technology. In a mature college administrative software market, software vendors have limited funds to upgrade their products. These vendors also face the inertia of a customer base using products that have experienced extensive tailoring to fit individual institution requirements.

A fourth issue is the Database Management System platform selection. The DBMS tool selected must have the features outlined in the above technology discussion. It should be selected from a company that is primarily in the business of building and selling DBMS tools. A DBMS built only for a particular application software offering should be avoided. Companies primarily in the applications development business do not usually expend the funds necessary to continually advance the capabilities of the DBMS tool.

The selection of a different DBMS tool will, in all probability, be required to implement the CWAIS. It is important to note that the skills of current administrative personnel in using current DBMS tools are transferable to the new DBMS tool. You don't need to take driving lessons if you sell your Ford and buy a Buick—your driving skills are transferable. The same is true when you use a new DBMS.

Issues Three and Four present an interesting dilemma. If the choice is to "make" applications software, the DBMS platform selection must be the first decision. All software is then built on that platform. But if the choice is to "buy" applications software, the first decision is to select the software that best satisfies applications processing requirements. The DBMS platform choice then defaults to the platform used by the chosen software.

The final issue is funding. An investment will be required initially to achieve benefits in the future. A new DBMS tool, purchased software, possibly hardware, and systems development personnel will cost money. A plan must be developed that will attract funding. A good plan will be successful because "money follows good ideas."

PAYOFF

As previously stated the campus-wide administrative information systems aims to *improve the administrative efficiency of the total enterprise.* The online availability of accurate information will improve the overall effectiveness, efficiency, and work tempo of all levels of administrative personnel.

The quality of work will also be improved by moving away from the current assembly-line process of handling information. It has been documented by quality studies that most people in a batch work flow environment spend 30 percent of their time correcting output received from others.

This improvement in efficiency, effectiveness, and quality will, in turn, result in better service to parents and students, the customers of the college. This high level of customer service can be provided at the lowest level of cost and thus improve the institution's competitive position.

Savings can be specifically achieved by eliminating time required to:

1. Create and send documents between departments.
2. Receive and process documents.
3. Input documents into multiple clerical or automated systems.
4. Process information through multiple systems.
5. Reconcile differences in multiple files on multiple systems.

SUMMARY

Current administrative systems are primarily department oriented. The systems are stable and functioning without serious problems but contain numerous inefficiencies. This discussion has shown that opportunities exist for efficiency improvements by utilizing the CWAIS approach in conjunction with new and improved technology tools.

Chapter Eighteen

DEVELOPING A PLAN

Michael F. Dieckmann
Director of Administrative Computing Services
Oberlin College

It is a sad fact of human nature that we seldom plan for the future when we find ourselves in comfortable circumstances at the present. Thus, when an organization embarks on "strategic planning" or "developing a vision," one assumes that the institution is under pressure, or that it sees a storm brewing on the horizon.

This fact is probably not a revelation to planners in information technology. Due to the explosive pace of our field, crises abound. (Indeed, when did we last find ourselves *not* in the midst of a crisis?) Often, in "solving" the immediate crisis, we merely create others to replace it, in a virus-like reproduction. We employ new computing technologies to solve existing problems, but these technologies often bring as many new problems as they solve.

Likewise, the issues we tackle now are more complex—the "easy" problems have all been solved. Our clients ask us to apply our tools and techniques to increasingly sophisticated situations. Our swords and lances are sharper, but alas, the dragons have grown bigger and meaner as well. Once we struggled to automate the production of an employee's paycheck; now an off-the-shelf $200 accounting package can perform that function for a medium-to small-scale business. Printing the paycheck is no longer our problem—instead, we now struggle to perform feats like integrating human resources information with the institutional planning budget and faculty instructional load parameters, while seeking to combine all data on employees, students, and alumni into an integrated database that is the heart of a campus-wide information system. Clearly, the scope of the problem is keeping pace with the sophistication of our tools.

Enterprise-wide computing is an area in which builders of information systems face their toughest problems today. Often the issues confronted are not merely technological, but encompass areas of policy and management. Perhaps nowhere in higher education are these problems felt more acutely than in small colleges, where pressures for institution-wide computing solutions are intense, yet resources are limited. The difference between a database holding records for 2,000 students and one for 20,000 students is more an issue of scale than of sophistication. The designer of a campus-wide information system for the small liberal arts college faces many of the same technical issues as does a colleague at a large state university. Although the information might be delivered to 2,000 customers rather than 20,000, the delivery methods tend to be remarkably similar, and the data items kept in the student records database for each student are comparable as well.

We do not minimize the computing problems faced by larger universities. Scale *does* make some difference, as do different types of institutional management and politics. Large universities face a diversity of problems and issues not present at smaller institutions. It is naive, however, to think that an institution of 2,000 students faces only 10 percent of the computing problems faced by a campus of 20,000 students; yet, budget and staff resources are usually proportional to student enrollment. This means that small colleges that strive to stay at the forefront of education find themselves—particularly in this day of shrinking budgets—having to tackle big problems using minimal resources.

THE ENVIRONMENT

Within this environment small colleges address their administrative computing needs. Many small institutions have not yet taken steps toward enterprise-wide computing, but are still dealing with mission-critical information systems in a piecemeal, nonintegrated fashion. Others use off-the-shelf solutions from various vendors: these institutions are being slowly pulled into enterprise-wide computing because vendors are moving their products in that direction based on integrated databases. Relatively few institutions are attempting to embrace enterprise-wide computing solutions via in-house software development. Oberlin College, however, is one that belongs in this latter category.

Oberlin is a small, residential, liberal arts college with an associated Conservatory of Music. Founded in 1833 and located in northeastern Ohio, Oberlin has an enrollment of approximately 2800 students, the majority of whom pursue either the Bachelor of Arts or Bachelor of Music degree. Although a small, liberal arts college, Oberlin shares many structural characteristics with larger institutions. A long-standing concentration on faculty research and scholarship leads to an academic environment more like a university than a traditional small teaching college. This atmosphere creates a need for resources to support the emphasis on research, including computing resources. The presence of a Conservatory of Music (in addition to the College of Arts and

Sciences) gives Oberlin a more complex administrative structure. Combined with a strong tradition of faculty governance, this situation both complicates many policy and procedural issues and also weakens many aspects of centralized planning and control. Thus, many administrative functions—including computing—are conducted in a more decentralized fashion at Oberlin than is typical of liberal arts colleges of similar size.

THE CRISIS

In 1989, Oberlin faced the pressures that spawned its latest information systems strategic plan. The events of the preceding ten years that led to "the crisis"—in themselves compelling tales of struggles and achievements, wars won and lost (often with heavy casualties on both sides), tragedies and generous serendipities—are not especially germane to the present discussion. In early 1989, however, Oberlin concluded a four-year conversion effort that moved all administrative information systems (over 5,500 software modules and 500,000 lines of Cobol code) from a defunct mainframe computer to a more modern minicomputer environment. As the dust began to settle, Oberlin found it necessary to pause and take stock of things.

Oberlin discovered itself the owner of a suite of aging and decrepit administrative information systems that automated only the most critical business functions. (The list of applications—admissions, student records, alumni and development records, accounting, student billing, human resources, and financial aid—would be familiar to anyone experienced in data processing in academia.) These systems blended a mixture of in-house and vendor-supplied products, all based on Cobol software and standard indexed data files. They existed as largely separate entities, cooperating in limited fashion along brittle interfaces prone to problems. With only a few precious exceptions, these systems fit the "legacy systems" stereotype reported in the popular data processing literature—old, outmoded and insufficient, but nevertheless the foundation of the business functions of the institution. Compounding the problem was the fact that these systems had remained largely static (i.e., without enhancement) throughout the preceding four-year conversion.

With this geriatric collection of information systems, Oberlin attempted to meet demands for the management information needed to face an increasingly competitive and demanding environment. Even with a massive proliferation of microcomputers on campus (to the extent that almost every faculty and professional staff member had a computer on her/his desk by that point), users of information services (IS) were extremely frustrated and getting more so every day. Facing ever-increasing demands from their own clients for information-based services, IS clients struggled with information systems riddled with deficiencies:

1. The systems had been designed to serve specific departments rather than the entire institution. Thus, it was difficult for some clients to get infor-

mation, even though critical to their business operations, that "belonged" to other departments.

2. The systems were built on outdated business models—some of them fifteen to twenty years old.

3. The systems were oriented toward batch processing and hardcopy reports, with little interactive processing.

4. Very little processed information was available—masses of raw data were entered and reported, but only in a few cases were data transformed into meaningful information.

5. The systems were inflexible and fragile. They could not adapt to a shifting environment as quickly as evolving real-world policies demanded.

6. There was little emphasis on historical data and long-term management information.

7. The systems concentrated mostly on tracking "this moment in time."

8. Combining data between applications systems for more global analyses was at best complex and frustrating, and at worst impossible.

It became clear to IS staff, upper management, and IS clients that a massive overhaul of Oberlin's basic business information systems was required. This realization, however, came to the fore at a time when the institution—like most of its peers—faced a host of intense pressures. Thus, the IS staff began to plan for radical change in Oberlin's computing environment at a time when the senior administration, preoccupied with other things, was unwilling to invest major amounts of time in developing an enterprise-wide computing vision.

STARTING TO PLAN

Principle 1: Strategic planning involves discovering where you are and defining where you wish to be, and then planning the journey from here to there.

The Administrative Computing Services (ACS) group of the Computing Center is responsible for Oberlin's centralized administrative information systems. ACS consists of a team of six software engineers whose activities are governed by a steering committee comprised of most of Oberlin's senior administrative officers. In 1989, faced with the adverse conditions described above, yet without clear directives from the administration, ACS reacted by doing something that was (to it) novel: it paused and asked "where are we?" Assessing the situation involved four major activities:

- Taking inventory of the current state of information systems technology in use at Oberlin
- Surveying and interviewing clients regarding their computing needs and frustrations
- Evaluating the current state and direction of the information systems industry

- Re-examining the basic mission and goals of Administrative Computing Services.

Each of these four activities was absolutely essential to the planning process. Knowledge of the present situation informs, *but should not overwhelm*, the process of defining what future is desired. In Oberlin's case, the main benefit of this knowledge lay in identifying specific problems, needs, and frustrations, and then looking for patterns and sources. Information from clients showed the depth of the problem, but it also emphasized how absolutely essential information services had become to the institution. Examining the state and direction of the computing industry allowed for informed choices of technologies to employ. Examining the basic mission and goals of ACS allowed the strategic plan to concentrate on the essentials of the vision.

THE STRATEGIC VISION

Principle 2: The plan itself is not nearly as important as the concepts derived from the act of planning.

Obviously, the key portion of any strategic plan is its vision of the future. Oberlin's IS strategic plan is grounded on a vision developed from an understanding of:

- The fundamental information needs of the institution
- A sense of the current state and general direction of computing technology as it relates to database-oriented information systems
- A vision of how computing technology can be employed to serve—and in some cases even enhance—Oberlin's business objectives
- A sense of the level of information technology the institution has the resources to support
- A sense of the level of risk Oberlin is willing to entertain; i.e., how closely the organization is going to chase the "bleeding edge" of technology.

As it devised a prototype vision of the future, Administrative Computing Services found it important to *ignore constraints*. Like the general process of "brainstorming," in strategic planning it is important first of all to capture ideas and possibilities, reserving for later the tempering of goals based on constraints and limitations. Several fundamental concepts emerged from this process:

- Institutional data must be widely available with the proper security controls
- Computing services should be delivered as close to the customer as possible. (For example, printing of hardcopy reports should be done close to the desk of the requesting client, not halfway across campus in the computing center.)

- Historical information is required for longitudinal analysis and long-term perspectives
- Enterprise-wide multi-client systems, highly interconnected through a central database, are required to support today's highly interactive institution
- Systems must be able to respond quickly to changing business needs
- Systems must be developed with a long-term view. Every use of precious resources in this massive effort must count.

With these principles and a sense of the general direction of computing technology as guides, ACS was ready to devise a more specific plan for Oberlin.

FACTORS INFLUENCING THE PLAN

Principle 3: All plans are formed within the constraints of a given environment. A plan that is well-suited to one environment might fail miserably in another, even though the objectives are the same in both.

Oberlin's strategic information systems plan is perhaps somewhat novel for a small liberal arts college; in many ways it resembles a plan that might seem more at home at a larger university. Several characteristics of Oberlin's culture influenced the plan:

- Oberlin has a complex administrative structure, many nontraditional programs and policies, and a very decentralized decision-making process
- Computing, particularly administrative computing, has long been a major emphasis at Oberlin, resulting in a larger-than-normal (for Oberlin's size) IS support staff
- Oberlin has suffered many bad experiences with vendor-supplied commercial applications software, usually requiring heavy modification of off-the-shelf packages
- Oberlin's administrative departments have been reluctant to modify their procedures to match the constraints of off-the-shelf software; rather, administrators expect software systems to conform to the constraints of real-world policies and procedures
- Microcomputers proliferated on campus in the early 1980s, so Oberlin represents a rich desktop computing environment
- Oberlin had already invested heavy resources in three major computing technologies: VAX/VMS systems, ORACLE relational database software, and Apple Macintosh microcomputers
- Just prior to the formation of the strategic plan, Oberlin had made the decision to move to campus-wide ethernet networking. Thus, a plan to develop the basic foundation of enterprise-wide systems—a campus-wide, peer-to-peer network—already existed.

ACS was charged with developing a strategic plan in an environment where commercially-supplied applications software had not been a success; where high expectations prevailed for customized, highly functional software applications; where heavy investments had recently been made in several key computing technologies; where plans for campus-wide networking were already in place; and where many obstacles existed to continuing pursuit of solutions involving commercially-available applications systems. Thus, the planners focused on a program of in-house systems development.

ARCHITECTURES AND INFRASTRUCTURES

Principle 4: Developing information systems is both an engineering activity and a business activity. Strategic computing plans must address both dimensions.

The basic outline of Oberlin's IS strategic plan was crafted by people who earn their livelihood by designing architectures for information systems. Thus, from the start, Oberlin's strategic plan was "architected"—that is, it displayed its own internal framework highly analogous to many of the technological architectures that it controls. Oberlin's IS strategic plan is founded on a troika of subplans:

- *The technology plan,* which describes the framework of concepts, policies, hardware, software, and methodologies used to implement enterprise-wide information systems
- *The strategic business needs plan,* which addresses institutional goals and priorities in scheduling the development of specific application systems
- *The computing services plan,* which describes the mission of Administrative Computing Services and the role ACS plays in deploying services that surround enterprise-wide information systems.

All three of these subplans are built on a common view of the various levels of administrative computing, described in an Information Resource Model (IRM). The IRM provides a method for placing information systems into a classification scheme that describes them as *enterprise-wide systems*, *departmental systems* (systems that serve the specialized needs of a single department), *special-purpose systems* (computing systems that are not general-purpose database-oriented information systems), and *personal systems* (systems that serve only a single employee and whose existence is relatively transparent to the institution).

Enterprise-wide systems are governed by the strategic plan; departmental, special-purpose, and personal systems are affected by the plan only where they interface with enterprise-wide systems. The technology plan addresses the engineering activities involved in building enterprise-wide computing. The strategic business needs plan and the computing services plan address business goals.

Technology Plan

The technology plan has multiple levels defining basic concepts, architectures, and specific tools. For example, a basic concept might be to deliver data from central servers to processes operating on desktop workstations. An architecture to support this would involve using a peer-to-peer campus-wide network. A specific tool or product to fill this need might be ethernet-based networking. The basic concept will be relatively long-lived, as might be the basic architecture (peer-to-peer networking); however, the specific tool (ethernet) may be replaced as the explosive arena of networking evolves.

The basic concepts of Oberlin's technology plan are to:

- House institutional data in an integrated relational database residing on central data servers
- Provide for widespread but secure access to institutional data via an enterprise-wide data administration and security model
- Provide processes that manipulate these data on both minicomputers and client workstations, using the basic framework of peer-to-peer campus-wide networking
- Distribute basic services, such as printing of hardcopy reports, to client offices
- Make systems interactive and screen-oriented, rather than batch and hardcopy-oriented
- *Empower end users* by providing services that enable them to perform a wide range of data manipulations without help from the IS staff. (Examples of these capabilities include ad hoc reporting and query, and natural language query of the database.)

The specific tools used to implement these concepts presently include ethernet networking, VAX/VMS central systems, ORACLE relational database software, and Macintosh client workstations. These tools may be replaced or expanded over time, while the basic concepts and architectures of the technology plan persist.

Strategic Business Needs Plan

The strategic business needs plan dictates the schedule and priorities that ACS follows when building new systems in the enterprise-wide framework. This part of the strategic plan is subject to frequent review and revision as the business needs and priorities of the institution change. In the first two years of the strategic plan, the business needs plan has been revised at least three times; yet, the overall strategic plan remains intact.

Computing Services Plan

The computing services plan controls how Oberlin will spend its limited human resources to support administrative computing. Oberlin is able to consider an ambitious plan for systems development because the efforts of ACS personnel are directed solely at developing and supporting enterprise-wide systems. Supporting departmental, special-purpose, and personal systems is outside the scope of ACS. Similarly, services such as networking and basic microcomputer support are provided by other groups within Oberlin's Computing Center.

DOES ENTERPRISE MODELING REQUIRE THE ENTIRE ENTERPRISE?

Principle 5: To be effective, a plan requires consensus; however, in the plan's development, sometimes lone rangers work better than posses.

Enterprise-wide computing is commonly defined as the development of databases and systems that serve an entire business, not merely isolated departments or divisions within that business. Thus, for example, an academic records system is no longer a tool merely of the Registrar. Rather, such a system serves the needs of the Registrar, academic department chairs, academic divisional deans, college administration, faculty advisors of students, and many others. It forms the basis of a campus-wide system that provides information on the course catalog, student biographical information, and the campus address/telephone directory. It communicates with systems that serve financial aid, residential life, health services, admissions, and alumni office needs. It provides data to a decision support system for enrollment forecasting and planning. It helps in classroom scheduling and faculty instructional load management. It reaches almost every corner of the institution.

While enterprise-wide computing has received a lot of press, the concept has matured just enough to show its many inherent difficulties. Normally, enterprise-wide computing is sold as something that must be implemented in a totally top-down fashion. Starting with the basic mission statement of the business, one works from the chief operating officer on down the administrative hierarchy to completely analyze the information and processing needs of the institution. Only when this monumental task has been completed can the IS staff begin to design and deploy databases and processing systems within that framework. In this approach, the task of enterprise modeling is primarily an activity of *analysis* (breaking the whole down into its constituent parts) rather than of *synthesis* (beginning with the parts and building up the whole).

The early practitioners of enterprise modeling report mixed results. A major complaint is the massive size of the initial effort to analyze the institution in a top-down fashion. Methods and tools do not match the problem. Most prevailing analysis methodologies—even in the wonderful new world of Computer Aided Software Engineering (CASE)—focus on developing static data and processing models of an organization. Unfortunately, the organizations modeled are far from static. This is particularly true in higher education; the university is the epitome of decentralized management. The result is that most enterprise-wide models developed in the top-down approach are obsolete long before they are completed, unless the organization is willing both to devote massive resources to the initial analysis and to freeze policy and procedures until the model is completed. Few institutions in today's competitive environment can afford this luxury.

Many look to new tools and methodologies—principally object-oriented techniques—to solve these problems and make true enterprise modeling a reality. There is indeed much promise here, but many institutions cannot afford to wait. Most of the computing industry recognized the usefulness of structured analysis and design methods in the mid-1970s; however, only today are CASE tools making these methods truly feasible. We hope not to have to wait as long for the tools and methods that will make enterprise modeling accessible to the masses.

In the meantime, those of us committed to developing enterprise-wide systems must struggle along with the tools that we have. In Oberlin's case, it became clear that neither the institution as a whole nor the IS organization in particular could afford a complete top-down enterprise analysis prior to developing new information systems. Instead, the IS group developed only the most basic model of the enterprise. Then, after designing a basic architecture for enterprise-wide systems, it proceeded with more in-depth analysis, design, and programming of individual systems.

Thus, Oberlin's approach began with only a moderate amount of enterprise analysis. The emphasis is on the incremental, ongoing process of synthesis that occurs when new systems are designed to merge into the enterprise-wide information systems architecture. A major benefit of this approach is that as a newly-constructed information system literally transforms the enterprise (often in unforeseen ways), the effects of this transformation can be taken into account as subsequent systems are added to the enterprise computing framework.

This "bottom-up" (or synthesis-oriented) approach, if it is to be successful, must follow certain precepts:

1. The analysts and designers must have a basic grasp of the institution as a whole, so that the information processing needs of specific divisions can be analyzed in light of the more global view; that is, a basic amount of up-front enterprise-wide analysis is still required.
2. The early development efforts must tackle the more major, foundational application systems that will form the basis of the enterprise-wide architecture. (For example, Oberlin's first effort was to design and build a biographic core database containing information about all persons of interest to the college. Subsequent systems such as student academic records, student financial aid, admissions, and human resources will be built on the foundation of the biographic core database.)
3. Information must be gathered from a wide range of clients, using high-yield, low-cost tools such as written surveys. Analysts must doggedly pursue information from key clients who at first might be unwilling to

respond. Likewise, the strategic plan in its early stages must be subjected to review from a broad body of clients.

4. The analysts must be able to combine departmental perspectives into an institutional perspective. A mechanism for checking the veracity of the institutional perspective must exist.

In Oberlin's case, Administrative Computing Services proposed an initial plan that addressed only the most global issues involved in producing enterprise-wide systems. This was somewhat of a "lone ranger" effort, using information gathered from a variety of clients through surveys and interviews, but involving planners locked away in the Computing Center. This embryonic plan was then subjected to successive levels of review and criticism from key clients, steering committees, and departmental and divisional managers. Refined at each stage, by the time the plan reached the senior administration it was ready for a consensus-building process.

The usual concerns arose in dealing with senior administration. Issues of budgeting, institutional priorities and schedules, balancing departmental needs against enterprise-wide needs, and "selling" the plan to various constituencies all had to be addressed. In Oberlin's case, however, we were able to petition senior administration with a plan already in hand, rather than the blank piece of paper that is usually the start of the top-down approach. This bottom-up approach would not be appropriate for many organizations, but it fit Oberlin's decentralized environment very well.

STRIVING FOR STABILITY; PLANNING FOR CHANGE

Principle 6: Systems and strategies, like living organisms, must adapt to their environment in order to survive.

When taking the synthesis-oriented approach to enterprise-wide computing, an institution must be willing to change previously built systems to conform to conditions uncovered in later development efforts. For example, in Oberlin's plan, the financial aid system was the first enterprise-wide system to be developed. While every effort was made in that system's design to ensure that all enterprise-wide data and processing needs were taken into account, it is clear that new requirements will be uncovered as related systems are built. In order for the enterprise information model to remain intact, Oberlin must be willing to change the financial aid system as required to maintain the integrity of enterprise-wide processing. Thus, we must adapt already developed information systems to new requirements that would (maybe) have been clear at the beginning in the top-down approach.

This situation represents, however, merely a special case of the general need for adaptable models and systems. Even in the top-down approach, analysts must still deal with a dynamic organization that strives to adapt to an ever-changing business environment. Organizations of the 1990s will undergo constant evolution. Designers of information systems must seek to produce systems as flexible as the institutions they model. Perhaps one day object-oriented technologies—or their children—will make this goal attainable. Until then, we must do the best we can using our limited tools. One folly that can result from an improper enterprise-wide modeling effort is an outdated model that no longer fits the current organization. An analogous problem occurs at the design and programming phases if systems produced are soon outdated because they cannot adapt to a constantly-changing enterprise model.

Oberlin's approach to this problem is to recognize that while the policies and procedures of the institution will undergo constant change, the basic data entities and services of the institution will not. A hundred years ago Oberlin dealt with prospective students, current students, alumni, faculty, other employees, donors, and the local and federal governments. It needed a method—albeit somewhat primitive—for placing students into a schedule of courses. Today, Oberlin still deals with information about essentially the same set of basic business entities. It must still provide the service of registering students into courses. The policies, procedures, and methods of registration have changed drastically during the current century. Nonetheless, the basic data entities and processing concepts have remained stable.

Thus, as we design information systems to serve Oberlin into the next century, we seek to develop a stable database model that will last for a decade or more with only incremental adaptation. We strive to implement as many basic business rules as possible directly in the database design rather than in functional system procedures ("code").

We design the functional components of systems to be as flexible as possible, using concepts such as data-driven processing. We identify short-lived "special-purpose" processes as opposed to longer-lived "general-purpose" ones, and we attempt to provide a clear separation between them. Yet, we expect to throw away and replace processes as required to meet the changing demands of the business. By consciously working to identify "islands of stability" in the information systems and separating them from the "sea of change" that surrounds them, we strive for long-lived systems that are as stable as possible.

This principle must apply at a higher level to the strategic plan itself. Basic concepts and goals of the strategic plan will remain relatively stable; many of the implementation strategies and business priorities will change.

INITIAL LESSONS

Principle 7: Plans are like children; in spite of their parents' best efforts, they sometimes wander astray.

As of this writing, Administrative Computing Services has operated for almost three years under a strategic plan which describes a ten-year effort. Various components of the plan have changed significantly since its inception.

Nevertheless, the plan has remained remarkably resilient, and the fundamental concepts remain intact.

Oberlin has found that the new technologies (relational database systems, fourth generation languages, specialized application-building tools) provide tremendous productivity improvements. Programmers accomplish now in hours or days what previously took weeks or months. However, the emphasis has shifted to the "up front" activities—analysis, design, implementation planning—for which few satisfying automated aids exist today.

It has required a major paradigm shift when designing systems to convert from departmental to enterprise-wide perspectives. Adopting new programming tools and techniques has required a major staff training effort, with a long learning curve. Developing a centralized, highly interconnected database has raised a whole new host of data administration concerns. (Once again, solutions create new problems.)

The separation of "stability versus change" has provided tremendous benefits; those parts of the plan that must be highly adaptable have been altered frequently in a three-year span, while the fundamentals persist. Shifting business priorities have altered the scheduling of specific subprojects, but the overall plan is roughly on schedule. The presence of a solid plan and a clear vision has vastly improved the morale of both IS staff and IS clients.

A strategic plan must undergo frequent verification. In the language of today's teenagers, frequent "reality checks" are necessary. Any long-term plan requires periodic measurement of progress against goals, reassessment of goals and methods, rethinking, revision, and adaptation to an ever-changing environment. The mechanism for this must be put into place when the plan is formed—indeed, it should be a basic part of the plan itself.

There is much truth to the notion that the act of planning is more valuable than the resulting plan. No strategic plan should assume a life of its own. An organization that is unwilling to revise its plan upon finding that it does not match reality is headed for a disaster; when the smoke clears, some new set of planners will be frantically developing a fresh plan.

THE FUTURE

Principle 8: Boxes come and go; concepts are longer lived.

Oberlin sees enterprise-wide computing based on an integrated database as the major paradigm for information systems during the 1990s. This model is fueling the rapid growth of technologies such as client/server computing. Also, new object-oriented software development platforms are providing significant advances in enabling in-house development of customized solutions. Just as financial analysts can now easily do their own "programming" using electronic spreadsheets, we see object-oriented technologies moving toward similar productivity leaps in building more complex software applications.

Thus, we remain confident in our decision to pursue in-house solutions for major applications systems.

The fundamental concepts of our technology plan remain constant, but we see changes to our tools over the horizon. Object-oriented databases will replace relational databases. An emphasis on the Macintosh workstation will likely be replaced by a multiple-client environment as a host of graphical user interfaces pursue common levels of functionality. Client/server tools will continue to replace our centralized, minicomputer-oriented ones. Proprietary operating systems will give way to more open systems. Hardware boxes will have ever-shorter life spans as product cycles continue to shrink.

Oberlin's goal is to maintain a strategic vision for administrative information systems that seeks the best service for the institution as a whole, using the best currently available technology, and grounded on strategic concepts that are based on a long-term perspective. This vision must be frequently validated with current real-world goals and practices. Although we have suffered our share of setbacks, to date this effort has exceeded our initial expectations. As always, the future will be our judge.

About The Authors

Robert W. Abbott is the director of academic computing at Bloomsburg University. He received his B.A. and M.A. degrees in political science at the University of Delaware. He has been providing support for academic computing for the last fourteen years. Formerly, Mr. Abbott taught political science at Norfolk State University.

Rosio Alvarez is currently working as a research assistant at the School of Management while pursuing a Ph.D. in management with a minor in computer science at the University of Massachusetts at Amherst. She has worked as a systems engineer for the Division of Student Affairs at the University of Massachusetts since 1989 and has been involved with all aspects of implementation and management of the student affairs division-wide network. She currently holds a B.A. degree in industrial engineering and operations research and a master's degree in business administration, both from the University of Massachusetts.

John Beckett is director of information services at Southern College of Seventh-day Adventists in Collegedale, Tennessee, a position he has held since 1977. He is responsible for administrative and academic computer services and telecommunications for the college and its associated industries. His previous experience was in FM radio broadcasting. He holds a B.A. in broadcast communications.

Dagrun Bennett is director of computing services at Franklin College in Indiana, a position she has held since 1974. Her responsibilities include the planning and management of academic and administrative computing services and data communication. She has a B.A. in information systems from Franklin College. Ms. Bennett is a member of the board of the Association of Small Computer Users in Education (ASCUE). She has served as the chair of the Administration and Finance Planning Group and the User Support Services Working Group of the Indiana statewide data network (INDnet), and is a member of the steering committee of the Private Academic Library Network of Indiana (PALNI). She has made presentations at ASCUE and other educational computing conferences.

Glenn A. Bieber is assistant director of computer services at Bloomsburg University. He received his M.S. in instructional technology and B.S. in business administration from Bloomsburg University. Prior to assuming his current position in 1986, Mr. Bieber spent four years with General Dynamics, Inc. as a project manager in the data systems division and eleven years with Mack Trucks, Inc. in various management and technical positions in the MIS department.

Michael Brennan is the systems software and networking support specialist for information systems at Pittsburg State. He has been with the university since 1985 and received a B.S. degree in computer science, minor in mathematics, from Pittsburg State.

Arthur Brooks has a B.A. degree from the University of Missouri-Columbia, 1965. He joined the staff of the UMR registrar's office in February 1967 as assistant registrar and has been involved with computing since 1967. Directly responsible for computing for the Office of the Director of Admissions and Registrar from 1969 to 1979, he has directed the transfer of the registrar's computing from the Rolla campus to central computing in 1970. In addition, he was a member of the UM Student Information System design/project team, 1972-75, and organized the first UM computer users group in 1976. Professor Brooks became the director of administrative data processing at its inception, in January 1979. He presented a paper at CAUSE 87 on purchasing departmental PCs from a campus time purchase fund.

Lloyd A. Case has a Ph.D. in theoretical physics from Brigham Young University. He was a professor of physics at Indiana University. He has taught physics, computer science, astronomy, and electronics at various universities. He published in relativity and in astrophysics. He has been the director of computer services at universities in Indiana, Michigan, and Ohio. For six years he was executive director in the University of Nevada system serving the state's two universities and five community colleges with computing and telecommunications. Dr. Case has also consulted widely in computing technology and telecommunications including many universities, colleges, college districts, businesses, state and federal governments, and the government of Egypt. He currently serves as director of information technology at the Stanislaus campus of the California State University System. The campus is located in Turlock, California.

Michael Dieckmann, a graduate of DePaul University, has been involved in computing in higher education for the past thirteen years, working at various times in academic computing services, microcomputer services, and administrative systems development. He has served as director of administrative computing services at Oberlin College since 1985.

Ray Grant was the associate director of administrative computing in the computing services department at Southern Oregon State College until November, 1992, when he became a self-employed consultant. He is now involved in a large project at Portland Community College which is implementing new administrative systems and networks. He has an M.B.A. from Idaho State University and has twenty years experience with computing in higher education.

Dorothy H. Hess has spent more than ten years in computing in higher education. She has been a director of administrative computing for six years. She has a comprehensive understanding of college administration and data needs. As a walk-around manager, while supporting college functions she uncovers situations and finds resolutions that prevent problems. With her skills in planning and analysis, she also assists other institutions in choosing new, or making better use of their current software and campus personnel. She currently serves as President of the international POISE Users Group.

Robert Keith has been director of information systems at Pittsburg State University since 1979. Prior to joining the university he worked in information systems capacities for Southwest Bancshares in Houston, Texas and the Bank of Oklahoma in Tulsa. Mr. Keith received a B.S. degree in business administration from Pittsburg State and an M.B.A. from the University of Oklahoma.

Albert C. Leiper is director of computer services at the University of New Haven, a position he has held for six years. He was formerly director of computer services at Greater New Haven State Technical College and has spent twenty-three years in Connecticut higher education, fourteen as a full-time professor. Also, Mr. Leiper has served as a consultant to local firms, including Timex Corporation. He holds a B.A. in mathematics from the University of Connecticut and an M.S. in mathematics from Trinity College, Hartford.

John R. Luthy became interested in computing after graduating from Dickinson College in 1974 with a B.A. in international studies. His responsibilities in the field of production control at an electronics manufacturing facility led him "to comprehend what computing could provide the decision-maker." His entry into the world of computing was as a would-be user. He joined computer services at Dickinson College in 1981 as a programmer/analyst and became coordinator of administrative computing in 1985. He describes his professional existence as "driven by the desire to see computing resources pressed into service to get the job done in the most productive manner."

Gary D. Malaney is director of the Student Affairs Research, Information, & Systems Office (SARIS) and assistant professor of higher education at the University of Massachusetts at Amherst. As director of SARIS, Dr. Malaney is responsible for coordinating all aspects of research and systems within student affairs. As a higher education faculty member, he teaches courses in strategic planning, research methods, and institutional research. He holds a Ph.D. in higher education and B.A and M.A. degrees in political science, all from Ohio State University. Dr. Malaney has over three dozen publications dealing primarily with student attitudes, enrollment management, and management information systems. His publications have appeared in several higher education journals, including *Research in Higher Education, The Review of Higher Education, NASPA Journal College and University, Journal of Marketing for Higher Education,* and *Journal of Educational Technology Systems.*

Dr. Lou Miller has an M.S. in computer science and a Ph.D in sociology. He taught sociology for seventeen years, first at Trinity University in San Antonio, Texas and then at Corpus Christi State University in Corpus Christi, Texas, where he was also director of the Social Science Research Center. Before accepting the position of director of computer services at Rollins College in Winter Park, Florida in March of 1992, Dr. Miller spent two and one-half years as director of computer services at the Population Research Center of the University of Texas, Austin, and served for two years as coordinator for computing in the sociology department, the Institute for Social Research, and the Survey Research Center at the University of Indiana, Bloomington.

Dale Nimrod is the director of the computing center at Luther College. He has been in charge of both academic and administrative computing since 1983.

Robert J. Parrish is vice president for administration and treasurer of Bloomsburg University. He received his bachelor's degree from Ohio University, and his master's and doctorate from Florida Atlantic University; he is also a certified public accountant. His areas of responsibility at Bloomsburg include telecommunications and networking, administrative computing, and academic computing.

George J. Sullivan is the acting director, administrative services and director operations and technical support for computing services, Rutgers University. His prior positions at Rutgers University since 1967 include associate director technical services, associate director administrative services, manager of university library computing, project manager administrative services, systems programmer and applications programmer for administrative services. From 1964 to 1967 Mr. Sullivan was employed at Bell Laboratories, Holmdel, New Jersey, as programmer/operator. He earned a B.S. in management science from Rutgers University and an M.B.A. from Rutgers Graduate School of Management.

Timothy Tracy graduated from the University of South Carolina with a B.S. degree in management science. In 1985 he joined the staff of Columbia College as assistant director of computer services. He is presently associate director of computer services where his primary responsibilities include managing the administrative computer system.

Glen W. Turney has over thirty years experience in the Information Technology field. Currently director of administrative computing for Kenyon College, he was employed by Rubbermaid Inc. for fifteen years in various information technology and management positions. Mr. Turney also served as manager of information services for Merril Publishing for ten years. He has a B.A. from the College of Wooster and an M.B.A. from Ohio University. He has also completed the advanced management program for the Case Western Reserve Graduate School of Business.

Thomas A. Warger is director of computing services at Bryn Mawr College, Bryn Mawr, Pennsylvania. He joined Bryn Mawr in 1986 and has held his present position since 1988, in which he is responsible for the management of academic and administrative computing and for the formulation of college policy in information technologies. Dr. Warger previously worked at Union College, in New York, where he was assistant to the vice president for academic affairs and also served as acting director of computing services. He holds a Ph.D. in French studies from Brown University and taught French on the faculties of Gettysburg and Union Colleges before switching to administrative duties. He is a member of the steering committee of the Consortium of Liberal Arts Colleges, the editorial committee of *CAUSE/Effect* magazine, and the EDUCOM membership committee. He has also been president of the Association of Small Computer Users in Education and a member of the DECUS refereed papers committee. In addition to numerous papers presented at professional meetings, he has recently written "The Organizational Structure of Computing Services," which appears in *Computing Strategies in Liberal Arts Colleges* (Addison-Wesley, 1992).

INDEX